D0311682

# THE POCKET GUIDE TO
## *Magic*

## BART KING

Illustrations by Remie Geoffroi

**GIBBS SMITH**
TO ENRICH AND INSPIRE HUMANKIND
Salt Lake City | Charleston | Santa Fe | Santa Barbara

First Edition
13 12 11 10 09    10 9 8 7 6 5 4 3

For a full bibliography for this book, please go to the
author's website: www.bartking.net

Published by
Gibbs Smith
P.O. Box 667
Layton, Utah 84041

1-800.835.4993 orders
www.gibbs-smith.com

Designed by Black Eye Design
Printed and bound in Canada
Gibbs Smith books are printed on either recycled,
100% post-consumer waste, FSC-certified papers or
on paper produced from a 100% certified sustainable
forest/controlled wood source.

Library of Congress Cataloging-in-Publication Data

King, Bart, 1962-
  The pocket guide to magic / Bart King ; illustrations
by Remie Geoffroi. — 1st ed.
     p. cm.
  ISBN-13: 978-1-4236-0637-6
  ISBN-10: 1-4236-0637-X
  1.  Magic.  I. Title.
  BF1611.K53 2009
  793.8—dc22
                                      2009009748

*To Luke*
*(go Trail Blazers!)*
*and Caleb*
*(go...juggling!)*

# CONTENTS

★★★

### ★★★

*Demonstrations of this book's illusions*
*are at* **www.bartking.net.**

## ACKNOWLEDGEMENTS

The gratitude I'd like to express to the following people is not illusory.

Caleb and Dave Sohigian, Luke Twomey, David Kelly, Amy Faust, Kent Meisel, Deena "Thimble" Stach, Michael King, Daniel Fredgant, the Celsi family (Rebecca, Ben, Eve, and David), Michael Milone, Doug Levin, Suzanne Taylor, Michelle Witte, and the staff at the Multnomah County Library.

# *Introduction*

Pick a book, any book . . .

### *"IF THIS BE MAGIC,*
### *LET IT BE AN ART."*
—*Shakespeare*

Congratulations! While there are more books about magic than any other performing art, you've somehow picked the right one. Yes, I've been practicing magic for literally minutes, and in these pages, you'll learn spectacular secrets that will . . .

Oh, wait, wait. Magic is magic, but there is illusion and then there's fantasy. While this book discusses wizards, sorcerers, witches, and the supernatural, it does not *endorse* them. Sure, it would be nice to wave a wand, utter a Latin phrase, and grow hair.[1] But I've determined that Harry Potter lives in an alternate universe, and so we earthly magicians have to create illusions with what we have: cleverness and sleight of hand.

While this book is about magic-for-fun, history is filled with examples of magic-as-fraud. The priests of ancient Greece, for instance, rigged temples with trapdoors, speaking tubes, and levers to impress visitors with the "power of the gods." Because of deceitful behavior like this, magicians developed a tradition of despising psychics, mediums, and spiritualists. That's because honest conjurers don't have anything to do with black magic or white magic. (But there is probably

---

1 *You're bald, right?*

## *Optimus Libri Umsom* ("the best book ever")

The idea of using Latin-sounding words ("*petrificus totalus!*") to make magic began in the time of King James I of England (1567–1625). A magician who performed for the king started each illusion with the spell, "*Hocus pocus, tontus, talontus, vade celerite iubeo.*" The magician's name: Hocus Pocus.

a green magician out there somewhere practicing eco-friendly illusions.)

Of course, magic DOES exist, and here's a true story to prove it: A man took his son to a play filled with magical effects. There were flying people and astounding disappearances. Popcorn was even available in the lobby! After the play, the boy said, "I wonder how they did that!"

The father began explaining how the flying actors wore special harnesses that lifted them up, but his son interrupted him. "No, Dad, I don't want to *know*. I want to *wonder*."

Smart kid! He understood that wonder, mystery, and amazement remind us of what a magical place our world is. And this leads us to an important question: Do you want to *amaze* people, or do you want to *fool* them?

Here's the difference: *People like to be amazed.* Perhaps you've heard of someone who's "*positively* amazed." That's because no one is ever *negatively* amazed! However, if you insist on *tricking* your audience, you might make them feel foolish. That's one reason why many magicians never use the word "trick." Instead, they use words like *effect, demonstration,* or *illusion*. And that's how you get around Jerry Seinfeld's complaint about magicians: "He comes on, he fools you, you feel stupid, show's over."[2]

Most people understand that the magician is an "honest liar"; his or her goal is to deceive the audience for entertainment. So it's okay for you to have an outrageous explanation of why your magic works. But claiming to have supernatural powers is pushing it too far. After all, the only real difference between you and your audience is that you know more about what you're doing than they do!

You want your audience members to drop their guard and appreciate your performance. How do you accomplish this? Make your magic as amazing as possible without being an annoying trickster. Because if you can get someone to *wonder* how you created an illusion, then *presto!*

## YOU <u>ARE</u> A MAGICIAN.

---

2  *Actor Jason Alexander (he played George on Seinfeld) is an enthusiastic magician.*

# *Hogwarts*
## IS FOR SISSIES!

**"BECOMING A FIRST-CLASS MAGICIAN CAN BE AS DIFFICULT AS BECOMING A FIRST-CLASS PIANIST."**
—*Robertson Davies*

Regardless of your age, you should be going to magic school.

"Why?" you ask.

You little scamp! Because it will make you a *better person*. And I'm not just pulling that out of a hat, either. Psychology professor Richard Wiseman

12

conducted a study on a group of British students who were sent to magic school. There the kids learned feats just like the ones in this book! And when the students were tested two weeks after their magic classes, the junior magicians scored higher in confidence and social skills than their Muggle classmates.

But what's so magic about *learning* magic? Professor Wiseman explained that students had to "have the self-discipline to learn the trick and think it through and look at it from someone else's perspective. They also had to learn to keep a secret while being likeable."

## Writing + Magic = Money!

In 2008, J. K. Rowling was the best-paid author in the world. She made $300 million over 365 days, which averages out to more than $820,000 a day. (Man, it takes me WEEKS to earn that much.)

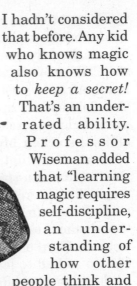

I hadn't considered that before. Any kid who knows magic also knows how to *keep a secret!* That's an underrated ability. Professor Wiseman added that "learning magic requires self-discipline, an understanding of how other people think and an ability to entertain. And unlike computer games it encourages children to interact with their friends and family."[1] In fact, the results of his study were so positive, Wiseman thinks magic should be made part of England's national curriculum!

---

1  *Marvin Berglas, the magician who taught the classes, added that magic is "both fun and cool."*

Of course, for you, the challenge might be in finding a good place to take magic classes. Luckily, you can always enroll at the College of Magic. (It's in Cape Town, South Africa. That's not a problem, is it?) The CoM opened in 1980 and is the only magic-training school in the world. It offers a six-year program in all aspects of magic. Beat that, Dumbledore! About one hundred students attend the college on-campus, and many others take online classes. If you're worried that you're too young (or old!) to attend, the college accepts any interested party from ten on up.

Is there a dress code? Yep! Boys have to wear black pants and a white shirt with a bow tie. Girls wear a black skirt or slacks and a white blouse.

These dress codes also apply to online students. How could anyone know if you were wearing the uniform or not? Don't make me say it.[2]

---

2  *It's magic.*

# Playing the Part!

*"A MAGICIAN IS AN ACTOR PLAYING
THE PART OF A MAGICIAN."*
—*Jean Eugène Robert-Houdin*

Steve Martin grew up two miles away
from Disneyland. As a young man, he
worked at Disney's magic shops. It was
there that Martin learned he had a soft
spot for performances that included
comedy. One of his favorite tricks went
like this: The magician strides forward
and announces, "And now, for the glove-
into-dove trick!"

The magician then throws a white glove into the air. The glove falls to the ground and lies there. The magician stares at the glove and waits.

Nothing happens. Then the magician goes onto his next trick, as if nothing happened.

The young Steve Martin noted that spectators loved this "illusion." He then theorized that the *lack* of magic could be entertaining because it was *unexpected*. Later, when Steve Martin went onstage to perform as a stand-up comic, he would use this strategy in acts like the Napkin Trick. For this, Martin would make a big show of unfolding a paper napkin, showing both sides, solemnly holding it up to his face, and then...sticking his tongue through it.

As Martin describes it, he concluded the trick this way: "I bowed deeply, as if what I had just done was unique in the history of show business." And while half the crowd might be bewildered, the other half would go nuts.

## THE "REAL WORK"

This reveals that a slick, no-mistakes magician can be *less* entertaining than a bumbling one. So how does a magician ensure that his performance goes as smoothly as he wants it to? Practice! What conjurors call *"the real work"* is the practice that goes into making the performance work the way you want it to. So start any new trick by practicing by yourself in front of a full-length mirror. This helps you see what your audience will see.

When you're ready to perform, get a "forgiving" crowd: Family, friends, and household pets are all good choices. THEN perform the effect in front of strangers. (When possible, select very nice strangers who don't know anything about magic but like the *idea* of it.)

18

*TIP:* Since virtually all magicians have good balance, dexterity, and hand-eye coordination, learn to juggle. Also, consider beginning a mixed martial-arts career. (This will be especially useful if there are any hecklers during your next performance for the local Boy Scout troop.)

## PATTER: TALKING THE TALK

When a comedian is onstage, he doesn't say, "What you are hearing is a joke about a goose." *He just tells the joke.* When a singer is singing, she doesn't pause mid-song to say, *"Look, I'm singing!"* So while you're making magic, try to avoid pointing out that that's what you're doing. And when you're performing a trick, don't explain *exactly* what you're going to do.

Of course, you could describe what you're doing *as* you do it, in case anyone isn't following along very well. You can also tell a made-up, fictional, and otherwise false story about the trick itself. ("A little old lady taught me this at mixed martial arts class...") This chitchat is what magicians call "patter."

## MISDIRECTION

Misdirection is what distracts your audience while you perform your "trick." That's why cheesy magicians wear cloaks

### Shut the Front Door, All-Star!

Near the end of a magic trick (especially if it's complex), it is a good idea to review the steps that have taken place before the crucial moment. As you perform, your audience will be thinking about all the possible ways you can pull off your trick. These are called "open doors." By reviewing the steps ("There was no way I could see what card you picked, right?") magicians "close the doors." It reinforces that what's about to happen is impossible, and therefore must be "magic"!

and have assistants who don't wear much clothing. But there are more creative ways to misdirect people. Take Penn & Teller's strategy. Penn would be onstage saying, "You only have one responsibility as an audience . . ." when suddenly Teller would appear at the back of the theater wearing a gorilla mask and smashing cymbals together.

Everyone would turn to look at him, and then back to Teller onstage. He would then finish his statement: "At no time allow your eyes to wander." (Too late!)

But having a *relaxed attitude* is just as good as a gorilla mask for misdirection. If you're at ease, your audience won't be on edge, waiting for you to "spring one" on them. Keep in mind that your audience will tend to look where *you* look, so if at all possible, just look *away* from anything you don't want them to notice. Further, any *big* move you make with one hand will cover a *small* move by the other. Sleight-of-hand superstar Apollo

Robbins insists that moving a hand in a simple arc (instead of a straight line) will always direct attention to it. So he distracts audiences by making arching hand movements with one hand while his *other* hand makes "magic."

But the best way to misdirect is to think about how to camouflage your INTENTION. If your trick seems to be about one thing, when it is ACTUALLY about another, you're on the right track! Let me give you an example, but first you need to know the *Rule of Three*.

Let's say a magician is tossing a ball in the air while saying, "I will now attempt to throw this ball so high that we can't see it anymore." She tosses the ball once. As it goes up, she keeps her eyes on the ball.

She catches the ball and throws it a second time, still watching the ball closely. (Studies clearly show that the spectators will probably watch the magician's face and then look at the same thing she does.) As she throws, she asks a question: "Do you think I can do it?"

But on her *third* throw, the magician only pantomimes the throw! That is, she makes the exact same move with her hand as before, and her eyes follow the path of where the ball would be. But there is no ball! The group did NOT notice the vanishing sleight-of-hand that she did with the ball. So, the two "establishing" movements—the question and the direction of the magician's gaze—all helped make her illusion work.

## PEN VANISH

You're up!

You know the disappearing pencil trick that the Joker performs in *The Dark Knight?* This isn't it. You just need a pen and a coin. Since you don't usually tell your audience *exactly* what you're going to do, make up something, e.g., "I'm going to change this pen into a pencil." Now turn to the side so that your audience sees you in profile. If you're right-handed, have your audience on your left. (Of course, you'll practice this in front of a mirror before doing it in front of an audience!)

Now hold the pen like you're going to write with it. Point the end at the middle of your left palm and you're ready. Bring your right hand up high and keep a look of concentration on your face as you gaze at your left palm. Bring the pen down smoothly and swiftly.

*YOU CAN USE ANY PATTER YOU WANT, BUT WHEN YOU FIRST PRACTICE THIS, JUST SAY, "ONE."*

Now do that again, and this time (if you're still practicing!) say, "Two."

The third time, look even more intent and, as you raise the pen, simply tuck it behind your ear. Without making a hiccup in your motion, say, "Three," and bring your hand down to your palm . . . and keep looking at it in a surprised way.

**YOU CAN END WITH, "SO MUCH FOR THAT TRICK. ANYONE HAVE A PENCIL I CAN BORROW?"**

**REVIEW:** See what happened? You gave misdirection, you used the Rule of Three, and you camouflaged your trick.

**ADD A TWIST:** Do the same trick, but this time, have a coin in your palm and tell your audience that the coin will disappear. Do the trick as described, but this time when the pen disappears, look confused and turn your body to the group so they can see the pen.

As they chuckle at your klutziness, you enjoy the misdirection because as you turn, you've snuck the coin into your pocket. Now make a fist with your left hand and keep turning back to your original position. Now reach up, grab the pen, bring it down, and say, "Three!"

Open your hand and the coin is gone too!

## GETTING CAUGHT

The potential for disaster lurks in all magic performances. But, hey, if you wanted to play it safe, you wouldn't have read this far! So if someone spots you palming a coin or footing a dollar bill, just smile and say that you were warming

### What Gorilla?

If you've ever watched someone walk and text message, you know people are bad at paying attention to two things at once. To test this, a Harvard study had volunteers count how many times one basketball team passed the ball. As they counted, half of the observers didn't even notice the person in a gorilla suit who walked onto the court and then paused in the middle of the action to beat his chest!

up for the really cool trick you were going to do next.

Then launch right into the Coolest Magic Trick in the World. (See page 143. My house is always set up for this trick. Yours should be too.) Magicians call having a back-up trick an "out." I call it a "good idea" so that you don't "take a Brodie."

*"TO TAKE A BRODIE" IS MAGICIAN TALK FOR FLOPPING. IT'S NAMED FOR STEVE BRODIE, A GUY WHO JUMPED OFF THE BROOKLYN BRIDGE AND LIVED.*

## SURPRISE!

The element of surprise is essential to good magic. Because of this, *never repeat a trick for the same audience* no matter how much they beg. In the words of Ukrainian magician Mr. Mysterio, "Not knowing what comes next in a performance of magic is where much of the delight lies."

## CRAZY TALK

The whole idea of watching a big "magic act" always seemed sort of phony to me. So I'd suggest that you practice a handful of tricks and get really good at them. Then choose when to inject a bit of magic and mystery into someone's life! It's cool to do an unexpected trick instead of trotting out illusions for people who aren't really in the mood for magic.

I guess that's it. Oh, how should you *end* your performance? I've always liked it when people end by raising their arms and saying, "I'm out."

## I'M OUT.

# Neat Feats

## AND FLORID FLOURISHES

> *"I KNOW THIS: IF LIFE IS
> ILLUSION, THEN I AM NO LESS
> AN ILLUSION, AND BEING THUS,
> THE ILLUSION IS REAL TO ME."*
> —*Conan the Barbarian*

Sometimes the simplest tricks are the most impressive. Take the police officer who accepted legendary escape artist **Harry Houdini**'s challenge to escape from his jail. The officer knew that Houdini was a master lock-picker who'd already escaped from the nation's

*See magic demonstrations at www.bartking.net*

highest security jail in twenty-seven minutes. Seeing as the officer's jail had an old keyhole lock, it was obvious that it was only a matter of *when* Houdini got out, not *if*.

Nonetheless, the officer put Houdini in the cell, closed the door, and went off to join some local reporters. The group awaited Houdini's quick appearance. Half an hour passed. They looked at each other in wonder. Two hours passed. By the time an embarrassed Houdini emerged, the reporters were astounded.

What challenge had this local jail posed for him? It was a simple one. The policeman left the jail door unlocked! Houdini tried to pick the door's lock, but the tumblers didn't move because *the door was already open*. And it took the world's greatest escape artist hours to figure it out. You've got to love it! But you are under no legal requirement to feel affection for the following simple tricks. These are good basics to know; they can sometimes serve for a quick solitary trick, or as a warm-up for a trick, or as filler between tricks.

## KNOT HEAD

Here's a feat that anyone can do the first time. Get a bandanna or towel or big cloth napkin (or anything like that) and place it in front of you. Now boast confidently that you can tie a knot without "letting go of the ends" of what you're tying.

Before anyone has a chance to consider that this is actually quite silly, fold your arms as shown at right and grasp the

NOTE: All chapters with activities start with the simplest feats and work to the more sophisticated. Oh, and feel free to twist the presentation of these tricks around to suit your needs and to better fit your personality.

two ends of the bandanna so that when you unfold your arms, you have a knot! Accept any of the coins given to you as payment to use in the next feat.

## PALMING

One key to being a magician is beginning to work on your *legerdemain* (le-jir-duh-main). This is the skillful use of your hands when conjuring items like cards, flamethrowers, and coins.

To get started, you need to know the Classic Palm. How classic is it? If you look closely at ancient Greek statues, you'll sometimes see coins concealed in their palms. (Don't take them or you'll get in trouble.) To practice the Classic Palm, get a coin the size of a quarter or bigger and put it in the center of your palm. You'll know where it should be when you slightly close your thumb; the ball of your thumb should push in on one side of the coin. Now slightly squeeze your hand and you'll find that the coin will stay there, but it takes a bit of practice. Try to keep it there without your fingers looking unnaturally clenched.

One way to practice this is to walk around with a coin palmed in either (or both!) of your hands. Think I'm kidding? Devoted magicians do this for hours. (Right now, I am trying to type and use my mouse while palming two coins. It's NOT easy— ^@jf-q-pwu31m. See?) Anyway, practice will help you palm coins and still look natural doing it. After a time, you'll find that while you're palming a coin you can snap your fingers or even pick up other items…like another coin!

Making your hand look natural while palming a coin is a good thing to practice. Like most people who aren't in jail, you will *naturally* look suspicious when you're doing the "sneaky" part of any trick. Practice looking innocent to help you deceive others in a bold, decisive way during your performance!

## FAKE PALMING

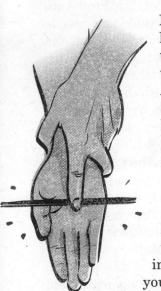

Now that you know how to palm something, you can *pretend* to do it for this trick. All you need is a coin and a pencil or butter knife, or any long object you can easily hold in your hand.

First, take the coin and quickly show your spectator how you might try to palm it. Put it in your palm, then turn your hand over, showing that the coin can stay there. Then hold up the pencil. "This is impossible to palm!" you proclaim.

Hold the pencil in your left hand, with the four fingers of your right hand wrapped around your left wrist. Now, quickly turn your hand, and as you do so, extend your right forefinger to hold the pencil in place. While you do this, act surprised and say something like, "Hey, I did it!" And it will look like you did. Don't hold this pose for too long, though, or it will be obvious that there is a finger unaccounted for! (More palming tricks are in the "Money Magic" chapter.)

## Act II!

Wearing a long-sleeve shirt, put a small rubber band around your left wrist. Insert a pencil beneath it; the length of this pencil should run down your wrist and under your sleeve. After doing the previous trick once, shake your hands out and try it again, but this time you won't use your finger to hold the "levitating" pencil in place. This time, turn your wrist as you position the levitating pencil and slide up the one held by the

35

rubber band so that the end of it presses *down* against the levitating pencil. This works so well, you could add a number of levitating pencils to the bunch; then at the end of the trick, grab all of them (including the one held by the rubber band) and lay them on the table. (This removes the evidence!)

## COIN ROLL

You don't HAVE to do sleight of hand to make magic, but, boy, does it help! Like legendary magician Jean Robert-Houdin (see page 195) said, *"To succeed as a conjurer, three things are essential: first, dexterity; second, dexterity; and third, dexterity."* Not only is rolling a coin or a poker chip across your fingers 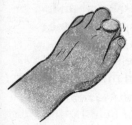 impressive, it's also good dexterity practice. And whether you're a magician or just playing cards with some friends, it shows that you've got skills. Mad, mad skills.

This is an easy feat to describe, but it does take practice. Start with a large coin (quarter or bigger) held upright between your thumb and forefinger. Using your thumb, push the coin up so that it lies down on the first joint of your finger. From there, you will use an up-and-down movement of your finger joints to move the coin across your hand. From there, it gets held between your ring finger and pinky, where your thumb retrieves it and you start over again.

NOTE: WHILE SLIGHTLY TIPPING YOUR HAND FROM LEFT TO RIGHT IS HELPFUL, KEEP YOUR HAND LEVEL FROM FRONT TO BACK WHILE DOING THIS.

Okay, are you getting the hang of this yet? If so, try it with your other hand. Now try it with both hands at the same time. Got it? Dig this: Expert prestidigitators can roll *two* coins on the same hand at the same time. As one coin finishes its run, another coin begins!

## THUMB'S UP (AND OFF)

Oops, I almost forgot this trick that kids love...or at least tolerate. Look at the picture below and then practice sliding your thumb back and forth to remove it and then reattach it. Once you can do it smoothly, you'll be able to remove your thumb without a hatchet very convincingly! (And if you can't do it, a hatchet is not included with this book, so just go on to the next feat.)

## STOOGE LIFT-OFF

A "stooge" is a secret partner, also known as an *accomplice* or *shill*. Any trick requiring a stooge will also require that there be at least three people present: *you*, the *stooge*, and an *audience*. And for this trick, you need one strong volunteer and one small stooge. Ask the strong volunteer to face the stooge. Encourage the volunteer to lift the stooge with his hands under her arms.

Once the lift is done, wave your hands around. (This is called a "flourish.") Then give a line of patter about how the volunteer can't do it a second time. Assuming the volunteer bites, this time the stooge should put his hands just above the volunteer's elbow joint, right at the bottom of her biceps. The volunteer will find it strangely impossible to lift the stooge a second time!

## IT'S IN THE CARDS

If you spent all your money on this book and now you can't afford a complete deck of cards, don't despair. You don't need a *full deck* for this feat. (Get it?) That's because before you learn to palm cards, hide cards, or make cards reappear, you should know how to THROW cards.

Big-shot magicians like Robert-Houdin and Houdini featured card throwing (also called "card scaling") in their acts. And although most card tricks work best with small audiences, Carl Herrmann and Howard Thurston entertained large theaters full of people by throwing cards, and this was often the most popular part of their acts! Both men could accurately throw a card from the stage to almost any part of the theater…including a particular person's lap.

To warm up, take a card and balance it on the tip of your left forefinger. Now set a quarter on the card, just above the tip of your finger. Got it?

40

Now flick the edge of the card with your right hand. The card will fly away, but the coin will remain on your finger!

Now you're ready. To get started with card throwing, take a card and clip one end of it between your first and second fingers. Curl the card into your wrist so that both your hand and wrist are coiled. Now bend at the elbow also, so that the card is curled inward to your chest.

The important thing is the card's release. When you throw the card, you will mostly be using your wrist and hand, almost all at the same time. It will be similar to throwing a Frisbee, but without following through with your arm as much. Snap your wrist fast and hard and keep your wrist even as you release the card, so that it flies out evenly.

Practice with short distances first. As you get the knack of it, try for longer distances by keeping the wrist-snap and adding more arm motion. You'll be amazed at how far a card can travel! Now that you're working on skills, try putting a hat or box five to ten feet from you. Practice throwing into the hat. Now you're ready for a target! If you know a fellow magician, have him stand with his back turned (or facing you, wearing goggles) and take turns throwing a deck's worth of cards at each other. Extra points for head shots!

★ THE WORLD'S RECORD FOR CARD-THROWING DISTANCE BELONGS TO MAGICIAN RICK SMITH JR.: 216 FEET! (OH, AND DO NOT THROW CARDS AT UNSUSPECTING PEOPLE. IF A POLICE OFFICER SEES YOU, YOU COULD BE THE SUBJECT OF A CARD-IAC ARREST.[1])

Once you can throw a card, you can boomerang one. Look at the illustration; with this grip, you are going to throw the

---

1  Oh, zinger!

card away from you, but only a few yards. And instead of releasing the card so it's even with the ground, now you want to release it at a 45-degree angle.

Practice in an area with a high ceiling and try to make the card spin as much as possible as it leaves your hand by snapping your finger on its corner. This spin will be what boomerangs the card back to you. It will take a little practice, but trust me, this is way easier than learning to ride a bike or blink.

*NOW HERE'S THE COOL PART:* Once you get the card to come back to you, you could catch it. But how about this: Hold the deck in your left hand and throw the card with your right. While the card is in flight, take your right hand and lift the top half of the deck up as if you were going to cut it. As the card comes back, move your left hand beneath it, and then trap the card in the middle of the deck by closing over the boomerang card with the other half of the deck! (This is difficult but possible.)

How cool would that be?[2]

## CLEAR A TABLE!

Okay, for the last neat feat, let me share that every time I pass a table covered with place settings on top of a table-cloth, my hands twitch. How great would it be to quickly SNATCH that table-cloth away while leaving the settings in their place?

But if it's just a regular tablecloth, don't try it. It'll be a disaster! (Trust me, I've tried.) No one is *that* fast, and there is too much friction with most tablecloths for this to work. BUT if you use a silk tablecloth, or another fabric that is oh-so-smooth, this trick IS possible.

The key is to pull quickly, and to pull the cloth straight out to the *side* of the table (without pulling up or down). Also, the heavier and more centered the items on

---

2  *VERY cool.*

the tablecloth are, the more likely they are to stay put.

Practice this trick with unbreakable items on a table. Since the unbreakable items may still go flying, do not practice this in an area with breakable items (like people) in it!

# Timeless Wonders
## THROUGH HISTORY

*"YOU CAN'T BE A GOOD CONJURER WITHOUT KNOWING THE HISTORY OF YOUR PROFESSION... THERE ARE NO NEW TRICKS UNDER THE SUN, ONLY VARIATIONS."* —Nicholas Barker

Teams playing for Tennessee's LeMoyne-Owen College are known as the Magicians. (And trust me, you do *not* want to go up against their Illusion Team.) The college's student handbook reads that LOC students "will execute their duties and responsibilities with resourcefulness and dignity, reflective of a true Magician."

Nice! Not only that, but at sporting events, the Magicians' rooting section shouts things like, *"Petrificus Totalus! Petrificus Totalus!"*[1]

Okay, I made up that last bit.

But what *is* true is that many people believe in magic at some level. Let's say you're playing Monopoly and need to get past Boardwalk. *Darned Boardwalk!* Before rolling the dice, you think it might help if you blew on them. So you do, and now you owe your little brother $1,000. Nice work! Anyway, magical thinking is when someone plays a hunch, follows his or her gut instinct, or acts on intuition. And it's been around as long as people have.

The first magic show that we know of was back in 2600 BCE. That was when a magician named **Dedi** performed for

---

1 *This spell temporarily paralyzes a person's body, as revealed in the Harry Potter books.*

King Khufu of Egypt. Dedi apparently decapitated a goose, duck, and ox, and then thoughtfully put their heads back on. (They were un-Dedi.) The Egyptians also give us the first records of both magic wands and the Cup and Balls trick. You've seen this routine before; three cups are set up on a table, and a ball is placed under one of them. The magician starts shuffling the cups rapidly, and although the spectators may THINK they know where the ball is, they are almost always wrong.

Meanwhile, the ancient Greeks also devoted special schools to the conjuring arts. Many Greek philosophers, like Pythagoras, were interested in learning magic so that they could become healers and receive helpful visions from the gods. The Greeks also devoted a goddess to magic: Hecate. She was the queen of all things uncanny, like ghosts, specters, and contestants on Greek reality TV shows. They also coined useful words like MAGEIA (magic) and MAGUS (wise man, magician).

The Greek historian Herodotus wrote of a Persian holiday called Magophonia, or the "Slaughter of the Magi." This was a day that no magus was allowed outdoors...under penalty of death! (This was their just punishment for coming up with those darned "Magic: The Gathering" cards.)

Next door in ancient Rome, performance magic was also popular, although magicians were regarded skeptically. To illustrate the point, the philosopher Apuleius wrote a popular novel about a man who travels far and wide to witness and learn magic tricks. The title of the book was *Aureus Asinus*. In English, that translates to *Golden Ass*. Uncool!

## Wrong Place, Wrong Time

In 1600, a Roman philosopher named Giordano Bruno asked if Jesus might have been a really good magician. For that, he was burned at the stake. (Today's visitors to Rome can find a statue of Bruno on his execution site.)

Another contribution to magic was made by a Roman named **Serenus Sammonicus**, who wrote down a method for curing fever in 208 CE. It looked like this:

```
A B R A C A D A B R A
 A B R A C A D A B R
  A B R A C A D A B
   A B R A C A D A
    A B R A C A D
     A B R A C A
      A B R A C
       A B R A
        A B R
         A B
          A
```

Notice that the ABRACADABRA is also spelled on two sides of this shape. The word was to be written on a piece of paper and worn by someone suffering from fever. Eventually the person would throw the paper into a stream and, as the paper dissolved, the fever would (hopefully) break. This method was so popular,

London residents used it 1,400 years later hoping to escape a plague outbreak. Over time, *abracadabra* became a generic word for a magical effect.

Because travel was relatively safe within the Roman Empire, magicians were able to tour and perform throughout much of Europe and the Middle East. But Roman leaders were not fans of *anyone* they thought might be able to put a curse on them or predict their fates. Even before Christianity took over the empire, the Roman dictator Cornelius Sulla deemed that any "soothsayers, enchanters and those who make use of sorcery" should get the death penalty. Magicians kept their illusions small so they could live to perform another day.

Europeans were unaware of the magic of the Far East until Marco Polo (ca. 1254–1324) returned from his travels and told of Hindu holy men he had seen in India. Known as *fakirs,* they had the uncanny ability to sleep on beds of nails, walk on coals, and generally withstand pain. Also of interest were the Indian street performers known as *jadoo-wallahs*. Their magic was often bloody, dark, and macabre. For example, jadoo-wallahs might pretend to cut out the tongue of a "volunteer" for entertainment. (Seriously.)

In contrast, magicians in China employed a refined style that qualified as theatrical art. China's influence on Japan led to the introduction of magic there over a thousand years ago. And so both Chinese and Japanese magicians learned elegant routines in which bowls of water containing live goldfish magically disappeared and reappeared, and sealed metal rings magically linked and came apart.

As for European conjurers, during the Middle Ages they had to be really careful. Any sleight of hand might be viewed as the work of invisible imps who were helping the magicians make objects disappear. Even non-magicians were suspect. In the thirteenth century, an English friar named **Roger Bacon (1214–1294)** took a great interest in the world around him, magic included. After writing about how magic-for-entertainment worked, Bacon was thrown into jail for fourteen years, and his notes were burned. As Pope Sylvester II learned when he was accused of selling his soul to the devil, nobody was safe. The Pope's crime? He was interested in science!

Even so, brave and greedy alchemists sought to discover the Philosopher's Stone, a device that could turn lead into silver or gold. (As a nice side effect, the Philosopher's Stone would also supposedly produce an elixir of immortality.) An alchemist named **Nicholas Flamel** claimed he discovered the Stone (also called the Sorcerer's Stone) in 1382. If so, Flamel and his wife, Perenelle, are still around today, but they didn't leave an instruction manual. Even without one, the experiments of Flamel and his colleagues led to breakthroughs in chemistry, medicine, astronomy, and other sciences. These new scientific discoveries eroded beliefs in superstitions and magic.

This helped make the world safer for entertainment magic, allowing **Franceso di Milano** to safely publish the world's first known book of performance magic in 1550: *How You Can Easily Learn Card Tricks*. And the world rejoiced!

As attitudes toward magic lightened up in the 1600s, fairs became extremely popular in Europe. These fairs were held on various saints' days and provided a chance to roll a market and a circus into one big event. They made an ideal setting for actors, contortionists, clowns, jugglers, and magicians to catch the eyes of passersby. And they needed skills to survive; the fairs didn't charge admission, so people only paid the entertainers who were *entertaining*. One of the best-paid of these entertainers was magician **Isaac Fawkes**. Among other wonders,

# Chess Magic

In the twenty-first century, mental magician **Derren Brown** simultaneously played a group of chess experts in the same room. Astoundingly, he beat four of them (including two grandmasters!), lost to three, and tied with two. (This feat is equal to playing one-on-one with nine NBA starters with the same results!)

To do it, Brown went to a board where he was playing black. The mentalist would then note the opening move of his white-playing opponent, whom we'll call Player I. Without moving a piece in response (thinking is allowed in chess!), Brown would go to a table where *he* was playing white and he would copy Player I's move.

Brown's opponent in that game, Player II, would move in response. Brown would remember that move, and when he returned to Player I's board, that's the move he would use! The games continued in this fashion, with the players *playing each other* and Brown just serving as middleman!

Fawkes presented mechanized dioramas like an apple tree that blossomed and grew fruit.

The interest in "automated magic" led Hungarian baron **Wolfgang von Kempelen** to invent a popular mechanized illusion. Called the Automaton Chess Player (a.k.a., "The Turk"), it was a chessboard built into a desk with the figure of a Turkish player at one end. The Turk moved his own pieces, and he was able to beat almost all living players who went against him...including Napoleon and Benjamin Franklin! The Turk perplexed Europe's finest minds.

Because it was so cleverly constructed, it seemed impossible for someone to hide inside it. But the gears and doors DID hide a person who moved the Turk's arms from inside the cabinet.

Meanwhile, folks in early America were not as accepting. In 1612, magicians (and other troublemakers, like actors) were banned in Jamestown, Virginia. Their banishment remained in effect for more than 150 years! How uptight were these people? Well, when a Massachusetts tavern owner announced he'd hired an entertainer to perform a few innocent tricks in 1691, a spontaneous public protest forced him to cancel the show.

## Revolutionaries Can Make Your Head Disappear

No magic trick could save **Chevalier Pinetti (1750–1800)**, the court magician of King Louis XVI. Imprisoned during the French Revolution, he received his summons to the guillotine while behind bars. With a smile, the brave conjuror said, "This is the first paper that I cannot conjure away."

As successful magicians strung more and more tricks together, they moved their acts from sidewalks and fairs to indoor theaters. With their formal expanded shows, magicians were no longer disreputable performers but well-respected members of society. Especially in the British Empire, amateur magicians were everywhere!

For example, **Lewis Carroll** (author of *Alice in Wonderland*) liked to perform magic tricks, and writer **Charles Dickens** was so talented that one reviewer suggested he could make more money from performing than from writing. Although he liked magic, Dickens despised supernatural fakers and spiritualists, a feeling that he had in common with a great number of magicians, past and present. One magician who went by the stage name of "Mysterious Smith" mocked spiritualists even while he profited from their reputations. Smith had a show billed as "Do the Spirits Return?" As he came onstage and addressed the crowd, Smith opened with,

"Ladies and gentlemen, you have come here to learn whether the spirits return. The answer is, 'No they do not.' "

Smith then did a magic show!

Slowly but surely, even Americans began to show some love for magic. **President Martin Van Buren (1837–41)** was nicknamed "the Little Magician," and **Abraham Lincoln** liked magic enough that he saw conjuror **John Wyman** four times. During the Civil War, Lincoln also saw Englishman **"Signor Blitz"** perform. Blitz had such impressive skills, he was willing to take requests from the audience. (Once, a Harvard student asked Blitz if he could "swallow himself." He couldn't.)

For his presidential performance, Blitz made a bird appear in Lincoln's famous stovepipe hat. The bird had a note attached to its wing that read, "Victory, General Grant." This referred to the Battle of Gettysburg, a battle that Grant *would* win. Impressed, Lincoln reportedly asked Blitz how many children he had made happy in his career. "Thousands and tens of thousands," was Blitz's answer.

"I fear that I have made thousands and tens of thousands unhappy, but it is for each of us to do our duty in the world, and I am trying to do mine," Lincoln replied.

While the Civil War raged in the U.S., visitors to London's Royal Polytechnic Institute got to see a ghost. That is, a ghostly figure appeared on a stage, walked through solid objects, and then vanished...right before their eyes! The illusion was named "Pepper's Ghost," after scientist **John Henry Pepper**. Thanks to an ingenious system of mirrors and lights, what *appeared* to be a ghost was actually the reflection of an off-stage actor. Magicians took a keen interest in this, and mirrors were included in endless stage acts, giving rise to the saying that magic is all "smoke and mirrors." (As illusionist Jim Steinmeyer says, "The same tricks that fool us today are the tricks that fooled your grandparents and their grandparents.")

As for sleight of hand, its greatest nine-teenth-century practitioner was **Johann Nepomuk Hofzinser**. One evening, the magician attended a high-society party in Vienna. As Ricky Jay (see page 192) relates, "an intriguing young woman was also in attendance, and someone remarked on the beauty of her teeth. 'Let me show you,' she said, and removed, one by one, the teeth from her mouth. The teeth were then placed in a cup and circulated among the confounded diners. Then Hofzinser made the teeth magically disappear. He then gestured to the woman, whose dazzling smile suggested those vanished teeth had miraculously been returned to her mouth." And this was how Hofzinser introduced his wife to Vienna!

# Harry Kellar (1849–1922)

**RESUME:** Kellar was probably the first great American magician. How great was he? Author L. Frank Baum based the wizard in *The Wizard of Oz* on him. And what an adventurer! While working at a pharmacy, Kellar was experimenting with sulfuric acid when he accidentally blew a hole in the floor. Instead of trying to explain this to his parents, Kellar jumped a rail car and ran away from home.

He was ten years old at the time.

The young Kellar worked as a magician's assistant, and he gave his first solo show at the age of sixteen. By the end of his career, Kellar had performed on six continents. Traveling the globe was quite an adventure; Kellar was robbed and even shipwrecked. He gave more than three hundred performances of his magic show in Philadelphia in the 1880s, one of the longest runs of any magic show ever. He also spent fifteen years in India and the Far East, learning illusions from fakers and fakirs alike.

*FUN FACT:* In Lima, Peru, Kellar was performing on a darkened stage when someone in the audience lit a match. After Kellar asked the person to put the match out, he was arrested! His crime? It was illegal there for a performer to speak directly to an audience member. Kellar should have asked the theater official (known as a *juez*) who was sitting in a special box onstage before doing so.

The total fine for that "crime" was about $1,600!

*QUOTABLE:* "Now we'll build a new one that no one will figure out," said Kellar after smashing a trick box with an axe when an audience member whispered that he knew how the box worked.

*TRADEMARK ILLUSIONS:* Kellar had a self-decapitation trick that was something to see. Nothing like cutting off your own head to get people's attention! Sadly, I am unable to share its secret with you. (You might get blood on these pages, and I cannot tolerate that.)

Before Harry Kellar retired in 1908, he named **Howard "the King of Cards" Thurston (1869–1936)** as his successor. It was a good move. In the early twentieth century, magic performances were extravaganzas, with outrageous costumes, multiple sets, and exotic animals in on the act. Thurston was a perfect fit. Where Kellar maxed out at five big illusions a performance, Thurston might do *eighteen*. In 1924, Thurston took his show to the White House to perform for Calvin Coolidge. He brought his own orchestra, twenty-two assistants, and a parade of trucks carrying his stage props.

Thurston's act was modestly titled "The Wonder Show of the Universe"!

He claimed to have been kidnapped by Algerian mystics when he was three. But the truth was that Thurston had been both a con man and a missionary before he went to see a **Herrmann the Great** performance when he was in his twenties. His mind properly blown, Thurston decided to become a magician.

Like many magicians, Thurston had a levitation trick. (There were wires involved.) Although he often invited children onstage to assist, Thurston's real-life manner was not child-friendly. A former volunteer recalled, *"As Thurston lifted me up, he said, 'If you touch any of these [expletive deleted] wires…' Well, I'd never heard language like that!…I opened my eyes and my mouth went wide, which made everyone in the audience think I was amazed at what I was seeing."*

65

## *Behind the Bamboo Curtain*

In 1906, Thurston performed in Kowloon (next to Hong Kong), but his Chinese audience seemed out of sorts. It was due to a culture gap; luckily, an audience member stood and requested that Thurston take short intermissions between his illusions. That way, people could discuss among themselves how each trick was done. Thurston agreed.

The show took five hours to complete.

Other magicians encountered similar difficulties in China. The conjuror Nicola decided to employ a Chinese interpreter to share the stage with him. But Nicola couldn't figure out why the audience was roaring with laughter throughout the program. Later he learned the translator was adding commentary to explain the illusions, like "There is a secret compartment in the box" or "The lady is no longer under the cloth, she is hiding behind the chair."

It turns out that Thurston cursed on the stage all the time. The magician uttered mystic incantations onstage throughout his career, but it turned out that the words were just a series of East Indian profanities!

Although modern magicians often write blogs, Tweet, and appear on YouTube and TV, Thurston was probably the world's first multimedia magician. In 1932, he became a star on radio, and NBC broadcast his fictionalized adventures. At that time, Thurston had already written and produced a stage play (*The Demon*), and he indirectly helped create one of the most famous fictional characters of the age: The Shadow.

Writer **Walter Gibson (1897–1985)** partly based the spooky superhero The Shadow on Thurston and his skills in creating dramatic illusions. (Houdini's escape artistry was another influence on the fictional character.) Gibson also wrote extensively on magic and was the

67

ghostwriter for magicians like Houdini, Thurston, and Harry Blackstone Jr.

**Harry "The World's Greatest Magician" Blackstone (1885–1965)** was probably the world's best-known magician in the 1930s. An animal lover, Blackstone liked to include his pets (including bunny rabbits!) in his shows. Blackstone was also known for his calm demeanor. This served him well during an Illinois performance in 1942. Blackstone was onstage when he learned that neighboring buildings were on fire. Fearful of causing a panicked stampede, Blackstone told the crowd that his next illusion was too big to be shown in the theater. He then excused the crowd, section by section, until everyone was safely outside.

Polish-born magician **Max Malini** was a magician with a gift for gab and an ability to do VERY long-range planning. His "gab" got him gigs with people like the King of Siam and President Teddy Roosevelt. His planning led him to have a card sewn into the lining of a senator's suit just in case he ran into the gentleman later. If he did, Malini could amaze everyone by naming the card and pulling it out of the suit!

## Rodents and Headwear

The first known "rabbit out of a top hat" trick was in 1836. So while Harry Blackstone wasn't the first, he was one of the most famous to lift a rodent from his headwear. The trick is almost unheard of today, but the image of a rabbit and a top hat has proved a durable symbol for magic. Maybe it's time for a new symbol. How about a guinea pig and a beanie? Or a hamster out of a homburg?

Magicians using animals must provide evidence to authorities showing the humane care, handling, and means of transport being used for these furry and feathered assistants. (Exceptions are made for manticores and griffins.)

NATIVE AMERICAN MAGICIANS WERE KNOWN FOR PULLING SNAKES, NOT RABBITS, OUT OF HATS.

In addition to being a terrific magician, **Dante (1882–1955)** was a showman as well. He made a point of staying in the finest hotels when he performed. Before going to his show, Dante would descend to the lobby in evening dress, silk-lined cape, and carrying a silver-handled walking stick. As he approached a taxi, Dante would call out, "Driver, take me to the finest theater in London, the [name of theater he was performing at], where the greatest show on earth is being presented."

Then he would catch his ride.

**Harry Houdini** liked to issue and accept challenges, and he claimed no magician could fool him three times with the same illusion. Years passed, and many magicians tried to make their marks by tricking Houdini. None did until 1922, when **Dai Vernon (1894–1992)** did a trick sometimes called the Ambitious Card. In it, a signed card is placed in the middle of a deck and then somehow rises to the top. Vernon did the trick for Houdini SIX times, and neither he nor the bystanders could figure it out. And thus Dai Vernon got another became known as The Man Who Fooled Houdini.

In some ways, magic hasn't fundamentally changed over time. But is there any place for it in the twenty-first century? Of course! The world's first TV channel devoted to magic was launched in the United Kingdom in 2008. And after magician **Steve Sheraton** saw an iPhone, he came up with a "magical" application called iMilk. This turns the iPhone into what looks like a glass of milk. Users can turn the iPhone to its side and "drink" from the top right corner, as if it were a glass. The milk then tilts and seems to pour in the person's mouth. Nice!

Yes, by seeming to break the laws of reality, magic will *always* have a place in our world, no matter who our cell-phone provider may be.

# *Secrets*

"Hey, how did you do that?"

You'll know your magic is working when you get that question. It means you just gave someone a feeling of wonderment. But if you then immediately *explain* how your magic is done, wonderment will turn into disenchantment in a flash. You're pulling back a curtain and revealing that the mighty Wizard of Oz is just a little man pushing buttons.

There's a word for giving away a magic trick: *exposure*. And people are almost always disappointed by exposures. Part of this is because most of a magician's "secrets" are simply stupid. Once you see how a trick is done, it's so simple, it takes the fun out of it. And then you feel stupid.

To cheer us all up, here is this chapter's finest joke on secrets: A cruise-ship magician presented his same show to a different group of tourists each week. Unfortunately, the captain's parrot saw the magic show over and over and began to see through the magician's misdirection.

The parrot started calling out things like, "Check the deck! All the cards are kings!" or "He hid the coin in his jacket pocket!" The crowd laughed and laughed, but the magician was furious. His secrets were revealed and his act was ruined!

In a fit of anger, the magician picked up the knife he was going to use for a later trick and threw it at the bird. The parrot dodged, and the knife bounced into the galley, where it made a spark that started a fire and set the cruise ship ablaze.

The ship burned to the ground (er, water) and had to be evacuated. Some time later, the magician looked around his life raft and saw the parrot staring at him from the other end. The bird clearly had something on its mind.

The parrot finally spoke. "OK, I give up. Where's the ship?"

So if someone asks, "How did you do it?" answer this way: "In your heart, you don't want to know." (Another possibility: "Can you keep a secret?" After the person says "Yes," say, "So can I.") Of course, it's an odd thing. You're willing to discover magical secrets because you're reading this book. Fair enough, some secrets are in here. But this is *not* the same as exposing secrets to people who are just curious about how you did *your* trick. Do they NEED to know how it's done? No! Showing them the secret will only destroy the magic for them (and for you!).

You may wonder if everyone already knows the secrets of all magic tricks. After all, many can easily be found on the Internet. But most people are lazy. Sure, they COULD learn the secrets of magic, but somehow, the idea of lifting a mouse and typing in a search term is just too much work. If people really want to find

In 2008, a group of almost fifty Japanese magicians sued two news agencies for exposing secrets of coin magic. The magicians claimed they had been "deprived of their assets," namely, the ideas of the tricks by the televising of trade secrets.

out what your secrets are, they can...so let them do their *own* homework!

And as for a book like this, forget it! An often-repeated saying in magic is, "If you want to keep something a secret, publish it." The magic secrets online and in pretty much *any* magic book are all common knowledge and/or public domain. As illusion master Jim Steinmeyer said, "Magicians guard an empty safe. There are few secrets that they possess which are beyond a grade-school science class, little technology more complex than a rubber band, a square of black fabric or a length of thread."

That's why I don't like TV programs such as the series *Magic's Biggest Secrets Revealed*. In it, an anonymous magician "defies" his fellow conjurers by revealing the illusions they worked so hard to create. How brave is this act of defiance? Well, the guy who hosts the show wears a mask! You see, the Masked Magician is afraid to reveal his identity.

Ooh, that reminds me of the story about a magical ass:

Magician **Charles Morritt (1861–1936)** invented an illusion called the Disappearing Donkey. Now, donkeys really *are* stubborn and hard to work with. In fact, donkeys used for this illusion have escaped entirely from the theater they were performing in!

So part of the drama of using a donkey onstage is in seeing how the stubborn beast will react. When magician **Edward Victor** did the Disappearing Donkey, the donkey refused to disappear. Conceding defeat, Victor turned to the audience and said, "I promised to show you a disappearing donkey, so I had better walk off the stage myself."

Then Victor exited, stage left.

# Big~Hair Magicians

Want to be a conjurer? Grow your hair long and then add lots of product to it! Yes, something about a big 'do seems to attract world-caliber magicians. Submitted for your approval are these two examples.

## Doug Henning

*APPEARANCE:* Henning didn't need a cape or a tuxedo. He had hair, and lots of it. His impressive helmet of feathered hair went with his tie-dyed T-shirt and coolio bellbottoms. But Henning seemed like a genuinely nice guy who was as amazed at his illusions as his spectators. This endeared him to audiences who might ordinarily have run the other way from the flower-power magician with the oversized 'do.

*RÉSUMÉ:* From 1975 to 1986, Henning was probably the most well-known magician in the world. In addition to a number of TV specials, Henning also had a Broadway magic/music show that opened in 1983 called *Merlin*. It had tremendous effects and outstanding magic, but critics noted three problems: Henning couldn't sing, dance, or act.

*FUN FACTS:* Henning ran for Parliament in Canada, promising to "make all of Canada's problems magically vanish by bringing the support of the Natural Law Party to the nation." Henning lost. Badly. Henning also claimed to be able to levitate through sheer willpower.

## David Copperfield

*RÉSUMÉ:* Born David Seth Kotkin and as a young man performed under the name Davino. Copperfield developed a theatrical (choreographed, even!)

style and went on to perform in many, many television specials. He's made so many millions of dollars, he was the world's sixth-highest grossing entertainer in 1995. Copperfield's already considerable fame was enhanced by his storybook romance with model Claudia Schiffer. (This was later followed by a storybook divorce.)

**TRADEMARK ILLUSIONS:** David Copperfield has performed many fantastic illusions. He walked through the Great Wall of China. He made the Statue of Liberty disappear. And he always has wind blowing through his hair…even indoors!

**ODD FACT:** After one of Copperfield's stage assistants almost had his arm cut off in a stage fan in 2008, the magician visited the man in the hospital and left him a children's magic kit.

# Money Magic

<blockquote>
"I DID A TRICK FOR A LITTLE BOY.
[HE SAID,] 'I KNOW HOW YOU DID
THAT.' I SAID, 'HOW?' HE SAID,
'YOU USED <u>MAGIC</u>.' IT'S THE BEST
EXPLANATION I EVER HEARD."

—Al Cohen
</blockquote>

Although coins are probably harder to work with than cards, they do have an advantage: they are MONEY. (Oh, sweet money!) If you have a volunteer and some coins lying around, we can do a quick trick right now. Take any three coins and put them on a table. Explain to your volunteer that you're going to turn your back and close your eyes. At that point, you'd like her to pick up one of the coins, look at both sides, take note of its year, and then hold it in her hand. Your volunteer should then concentrate and visualize both sides of the coin. Finally, she should return the coin to the table with the others and tell you she's done.

You will turn and ask her to keep thinking of the coin. As she does, you need to quickly touch each of the coins. Which one is warmest? That's the one she had in her hand! Oh, and once you know which coin it is, don't announce the right one immediately.

Since you have a volunteer, try this bit of silliness. Take one of the coins and hold it up. Have your volunteer open her hand, palm outstretched, and, with a flourish, push the coin into her palm and tell her to close her hand into a tight fist around it.

After she does, say, "Would you be surprised if I could take it out of your hand?" No matter what your volunteer says, add, "Please open your hand." Even if the volunteer is skeptical, she will open her hand to check if the coin is there. It is, which is why you quickly take it and say, "Thank you very much."

Zinger!

## Travel Expenses

James "the Amazing" Randi was once impressed by a Japanese salesman who pulled a five-hundred-yen note out of his pocket, unfolded it with a flourish, and set it on the table. The money started walking away! The salesman then turned the bill around and it walked toward him. He set the bill against the wall and it walked up the wall! Randi was flabbergasted until he learned the man had glued a cockroach to the back of the yen note.

Coin magic often involves making coins *disappear*, and herein is one of the cardinal rules of magic: When you see a magician "disappear" something, it either was never there in the first place, or it's STILL there and you just think it's gone. So let's try the easiest way of making something disappear: using a stooge!

## MISSION: ACCOMPLICE

All you need for this trick are two coins and a cloth napkin or handkerchief or T-shirt (or any other covering!). You will also need a stooge, and in this description, I'm imagining two additional audience members.

Set one coin in front of you and one coin in the middle of the table. With a suspicious flourish or two, lay the napkin over the coin in the middle. Make a few passes, and have an audience member reach under the napkin to see if the coin is still there. (It will be.) Cast another spell and have the next audience member check on the coin. It will still be there! One more spell, and have the stooge check on the coin. The stooge will *say* the coin is still there.

"Darn it!" you cry. "My magic's date has expired." You lift the napkin in disgust, only to find the coin is actually gone! You express delight that the magic worked and the audience is amazed. Oh, and let your accomplice keep the coin, by the way. After all, he helped with the trick by taking the coin and then saying it was still there!

### Act II: Lap Dropping (No Accomplice!)

If you're paying attention, there's still another coin in front of you. Now if the trick you just did worked, say, "Let's try that again." (If it didn't work, say the same thing!)

*OPTION A:* Reach for the coin with your right hand and, as you do so, form a loose fist with your left hand at the edge of the table. This will form a funnel, and the bottom of your fist should be just off the table.

Take the coin and drop it into your fist. As the coin passes your first finger, close the top of your fist but leave the bottom open for an instant. (The coin will drop into your lap.) Then bring your left hand up and act surprised that the coin is gone!

*OPTION B:* With the coin in front of you, cover it with your right hand, and begin dragging it toward the edge of the table. As you get to the edge, the coin will drop into your lap, but you will *pretend* to have it just beneath your forefinger, index finger, and thumb. Be smooth; do not pause or hesitate! Place the imaginary coin in your left palm and let your left hand close around it. Then open your left hand to show that it's gone!

## THE FRENCH DROP

You already know the **Classic Palm** from page 32. The French Drop is another coin trick where you seem to take a coin but actually don't. Hold the coin with your left hand as shown by the illustration. As your right hand approaches, you are going

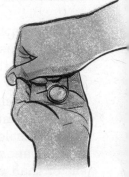

to PRETEND to take the coin. But instead of doing so, you'll have your right hand clench over the coin and then you'll "drop" it into your left palm.

In a perfect world, you'll be able to grip the coin in a Classic Palm. Or you may simply let the coin fall inside the curled fingers of your hand, resting against the top of your palm. (This is known as a "finger palm." See page 90.) Either way, let your left hand swing to your side while you maintain your focus on your *right* hand. Pretend the coin really is in that hand. Then you open it, but, hey—there's no coin there!

At this point, you should have the actual coin in a Classic Palm. That way you can just hold it there for a moment without immediately sticking your hand in your pocket, which tends to be a giveaway. If someone thinks the coin is there, reach the hand holding the coin up to the skeptic's ear and pull it out of there! This is easier than you think, especially if you have the coin finger-palmed. Just keep it concealed as your hand goes up. Maintain eye contact, and once you're by the person's ear, push the coin forward with your thumb while simulating a picking motion. Brush his earlobe and then produce the coin from your palm with an "Ah ha!"

*TIP:* To enhance your fakery, note the date on a coin you will be using for a trick. After making a fake switch, conceal the imaginary coin in your hand and "read" its date aloud! You can later "prove" it actually WAS there by having someone check the date.

## THE FINGER PALM

Another good feat to know is the **Fake Placement**. Start with the coin in your right hand. Use a finger palm, as shown in the illustration below. Clench your fingers a little and use your pinky to support and cup the side of the coin as you turn your hand over to seemingly dump it into your other palm.

As you move your right hand (still holding the coin!) away, extend your forefinger to point at your left hand. Yep, that's misdirection. As your right hand hangs at your side, you squeeze your left hand, and then open it up, amazed!

As before, if someone suspects there's something hidden in your right hand, pull a coin out of that person's ear. Even better: complain about your sinuses and bring your right hand up and cup it around your nose. Then blow! The coin will come flying out, and everyone will think you have a mint in your schnozz. (I always wanted to write that.)

## JUMPIN' JEHOSAPHAT

This is such a simple disappearing trick, you won't believe it works. After a minute of practice, you'll think it's impossible. But after three minutes of practicing it, you'll jump for joy at its beauty.

You need to be seated at a table. Hold a coin in the palm of each hand. Put the coin in your left hand under your ring finger, while the one in your right hand is under your forefinger and index finger. Now, flip both of your hands downward! But each hand should move a little differently. With your right hand, you are flipping the coin to your left. With your left hand, you are cupping the coin that's there and catching the incoming one. Seriously, practice this twenty times and you'll be surprised at how quickly and well you can do it.

## FAST MONEY!

### Act I

Get a fresh bill and fold it lightly lengthwise. Present it to your volunteer and tell him that he can have the bill if he can catch it as it falls. He will be excited, but rest easy. Have the person hold his fist out. He then needs to stick out his thumb and forefinger because he will try to catch the bill by pinching it between these two fingers.

Make sure your fingers are dry and hold the bill halfway between the person's thumb and finger. Tell the person that he can't drop his hand down in the air to catch the bill; his arm *must* remain motionless. Then release the bill. He'll miss it. Go ahead and do it again, but now as you hold the bill between his fingers, talk a little bit to throw him off guard and then release the bill. It is almost impossible for someone to grab the bill because it falls beyond his grasp in one-fifth of a second. Most people can't react that fast!

## Act II

Since you already have a bill, get two paperclips and a rubber band for the next trick. Fold one bill a third of the way back on itself and clip it there. Now put the rubber band around the note at the halfway point.
Finally, fold the other third of the bill in the opposite direction and clip it as the illustration shows. (It should be clipped to the top of the fold you made earlier.)

Now you're ready! Grab both ends of the bill and pull on the ends until the bill is flat. You'll magically end up with the two paperclips clipped together and dangling from the rubber band! Do this slowly the first time and experiment with speed to see how to make it look most impressive.

## RUBBER BANDIT

To do this coin trick, you need a coin and a small rubber band. You also need a bandanna, a cloth napkin, or even a shirt. (If the cloth has any pattern on it, so much the better.) Put the rubber band in your pocket and you're ready!

Hold up the cloth, showing that there is nothing unusual to it. You might even let your subject investigate it, and as he does so, you reach into your pocket and get the rubber band. Take the cloth back, and as your hand holding the rubber band emerges from your pocket, cover it with the cloth.

Now, while your hand is under there, wrap the rubber band around the outside of your fingers. With your other hand, take a coin and hold it up for inspection. Take the coin and push it into your outstretched fingers inside the bandanna. While you're doing this, let the rubber band around your fingers close over the top of the quarter from under the bandanna. With the coin trapped inside the bandanna, grab the edge of it with your free hand and pull it away. There's no coin! And as long as you don't show the backside, the illusion will remain. (But just to make sure, put the bandanna in your pocket.)

## STACKS OF MONEY

For this, make the bold pronouncement that you can balance a coin on a dollar. Or meekly wonder if you can balance a coin on a dollar. Either way, you're going to balance a coin on a dollar!

First, any paper money from any country will do. But it needs to be new, crisp, fresh money! If you've got that covered, take a bill and fold it once, perfectly in half along its length. This and the fold that follows need to be good, sharp creases. Next, take the creased bill and fold it perfectly along its width. Then, place the note on a table with the folded edges facing up, so that it forms a "V" shape. (The bill should be able to stand on its own.)

Place the coin at the intersection of the "V" and let it rest there. Then carefully grip the ends of the bill and start straightening it out into a line. If done properly, the coin will find its own equilibrium and will impossibly perch right on the edge of your dollar!

# *Druids*

*RÉSUMÉ:* More than two thousand years ago, the Druids were the people to see for tips on gardening and human sacrifice. In the ancient Celtic religion, the Druids wore many hoods, serving as combination priests/politicians/magicians. From their power base in what's now France and Britain, the Druids oversaw religious practices, settled disputes, and had seemingly magical abilities.

*PHILOSOPHY:* The Druids draped themselves in so many long robes and mysteries, it's almost impossible for us to know what's Druid legend and what's Druid fact.

*HOBBIES:* One thing we ARE sure about is that the Druids liked to make giant wicker baskets. It was a fun craft project that all the Druids could work on together! Then they would fill the giant wicker baskets with criminals and set them on fire. Not enough criminals around to fill the basket? Recruit a few innocent people! This practice took the fun out of picnic baskets for millennia.

*QUOTABLE:* "Who brought the matches?"

*COMING UN-HENGED:* While Stonehenge was long believed to be a Druid hangout, it's at odds with their usual style. Druids typically had "services" in cleared glades deep in the forest. And as far as we know, they didn't cart giant stones about for their ceremonies. But maybe they did so for their cemeteries because experts agree that Stonehenge was used as a burial ground from its very beginning…five

98

thousand years ago!

*TRADEMARK ILLUSION:* Many communities served by the Druids had no written language. So by knowing what a calendar was, the Druids could "magically" forecast the weather and seasons to some extent.

*BURN ON YOU:* When the ancient Romans conquered Druid turf, they found these forest priests obnoxious and barbaric. Why set giant wicker baskets on fire when you could crucify someone? After the Roman Empire, the vestiges of Druidism were wiped out by Christians, who didn't approve of pagan rituals. And they'd burn any Druid at the stake who disagreed!

*BEWARE!* Druids still exist, and they are itching for some payback. Avoid overnight camping trips in haunted forests and the food court at the mall. (Druids LOVE the food court.)

# *Diabolical Magic* OF THE BLACKEST SORT

### *"LISTEN, IF BEING EVIL WAS EASY, EVERYONE WOULD DO IT."*
—*Neil Zawacki*

"Black magic" usually refers to supernatural magic intended for evil purposes. That means that a black magic trick might start this way: "Pick a card, any card. Got one? Good. Now look at the card and remember what it is *while you burn in fire for all eternity!*"

Oh, that's rich—hang on while I wipe my eyes...Okay, I'm back. Whew! People have not been very good at telling the difference between *black* magic and the *honest* magic magicians use to entertain an audience. And so, throughout history, most of the people accused of using black magic were either curious folks conducting scientific experiments or innocent victims of persecution. ("*She wouldn't give me a carrot. Witch!*") Of course, there have been a few power-mad dolts who really did want to awaken an Evil Power and then conquer the world. But ponder this: How fun could it be to rule a smoldering planet inhabited by zombies?

Black magic men and women go way back. In ancient Babylonia, we find the first references to dark sorcerers who could be hired to put a curse on one's nemesis (ineffective), raise a dead spirit (ineffective), or poison a hated enemy (effective!). Fast-forwarding, between 500 and 1100 CE, Europeans found black magic especially troubling. You'd think they would've been tolerant of *black* magic because it was the *Dark* Ages. But no! Instead,

## Giving in to the Dark Side?

Are you worried that you may be transforming from an innocent conjurer into a dark necromancer? Look for these warning signs:

★ YOUR STAGE PATTER TURNS UGLY, E.G., "THANK YOU. YOUR APPLAUSE MAKES ME FEEL ALL WARM AND FUZZY INSIDE, LIKE I SWALLOWED A KITTEN."

★ YOU PREFER BLACK MAGIC MARKERS TO FINE-TIP BALLPOINTS.

★ YOU DEAL WITH HECKLERS BY SUMMONING DEMONS.

★ INSTEAD OF A CUP-AND-BALLS PERFORMANCE, YOU FIND YOURSELF DOING A CUP-AND-SHRUNKEN-HEAD ROUTINE.

★ YOU'RE SO UPSET THAT YOUR LOCAL LIBRARY DOESN'T STOCK <u>THE BOOK OF EVIL</u> THAT YOU SEND A ZOMBIE ARMY TO ATTACK IT. (HELPFUL TIP: WHILE THEY'RE THERE, HAVE THE ZOMBIES PAY YOUR OVERDUE FINES.)

★ YOUR "BURYING SOMEONE ALIVE" ILLUSION IS <u>NOT</u> AN ILLUSION.

they constantly fussed over nonsense like witchcraft and demons. As many as 150,000 women were burned at the stake by the end of the Middle Ages just because they were *suspected* of being witches.

And what's the story with the broom-sticks? Is housework evil? It's believed that brooms are associated with witches because farmwomen would sometimes "ride" broomsticks through fields that had been planted. They did this because brooms were associated with women, and women were fertile. So brooms were symbols of fertility too, and when "ridden" over the fields, it was thought the brooms would help the crops grow.

In the 1200s, **Pope Gregory IX** founded a little something called the Inquisition. This was a campaign against people who disagreed with Christian beliefs that became famous for its use of torture to get confessions from witches, sorcerers, and jaywalkers. Two Germans assisting with the Inquisition wrote the medieval bestseller *Malleus Maleficarum* (*The Hammer of Witches*) in 1486. Their book laid out what witches were up to and gave handy tips on the best ways to torture them. It's pretty brutal; the best description is that it's a guide to "judicial murder." Over the next two hundred years, the only book that sold better than the *Malleus* was *The Bible*.

It was very unhelpful that books of spells called *grimoires* (grim-wars) began popping up. The grimoires were written by anonymous authors and contained procedures that supposedly raised demons and other unsavory activities. Of course, this just made people even more paranoid

## Judge, Jury, Executioner

If a witch were found guilty and executed, her possessions were split between the Inquisitors, the royal treasury, and the Catholic Church. That's three reasons for a guilty verdict!

about black magic. And so even into the 1600s, "witches" suffered fiery fates in the bonfires of fanatics.

It wasn't only women who suffered. The French scholar named **Heinrich Agrippa (1486–1535)** was an impressive man who spoke eight languages and was a doctor and a lawyer. But after he published a three-volume set titled *De Occulta Philosophia* (*Occult Philosophy*), none of that mattered. Even though the books just suggested that nature contained unknown mysteries, Agrippa's enemies captured and tortured him. He died shortly thereafter.

But Agrippa's reputation lived on. You may be familiar with his name because he was on Ron Weasley's missing Chocolate Frogs card. Also, in the mid-1800s, a mental hospital director named **Heinrich Hoffman** wrote a children's book called *Strewwelpeter* (*Sloppy Peter*). In it, Peter and other young characters are naughty and then are injured, mutilated, or killed by characters like the evil Agrippa. (*Moral*: Don't let mental hospital directors write books for children.)

Another superstar of the dark arts was **Michel de Nostradamus**. Born in France in 1503, Nostradamus was a doctor who lost his wife and two children to the plague. This tragedy inspired Nostradamus to write. Over nearly twenty years, he wrote poems, a handbook about jelly, and prophecies. (None of his prophecies had to do with jelly.) For example:

*THE YOUNG LION SHALL OVERCOME THE OLD*
*ON FIELD OF WAR IN SINGLE COMBAT*
*IN A CAGE OF GOLD HIS EYE SHALL BE PIERCED*
*TWO KNELLS FOR ONE,*
*THEN DIE A CRUEL DEATH.*

Shortly after this was printed, the French king, **Henry II**, took part in a jousting tournament. A lance broke on his golden helmet, pierced his eye, and killed him. From then on, Nostradamus's reputation was so good that his fans today insist that Nostradamus also predicted World War II, nuclear weapons, and the Great Cheese Whiz Disaster of 2008.

While Nostradamus was writing poems, an Englishman named **Reginald Scot** saw a woman accused of witchcraft for doing a simple sleight-of-hand trick. Scot tried to set matters straight with his 1584 book *The Discoverie of Witchcraft*. In it, Scot described the tricks that street performers used so he could contrast legitimate magicians from black magic sorcerers. Nice try! But **King James I** ordered all copies of Scot's book seized and (surprise!) burned. This was good marketing, as King James' own book (a defense of witch hunting titled *Demonologie*) became a best seller!

Part of the misunderstanding was that, at that time, any phenomenon that wasn't completely understood was credited to either God or the devil. Since only a blessed person or saint could perform one of God's miracles, that left ALL other

## *I Like Vanilla!*

A *theurgist* is someone skilled in *white* magic. (You know, like Saruman before his make-over.)

unexplained events to the devil! And so as recently as the 1800s, magician **M. Comte** nearly got thrown into a fiery charcoal pit in Switzerland. (His audience was convinced he was talking with demons after he did some ventriloquism tricks.)

Just as the townspeople were getting ready to toss him in, a voice from the fire-pit intoned that if any harm came to the magician, they would all roast in hell. The mob dropped Comte and ran off, leaving him to consider how ventriloquism got him *into* and *out of* a hot spot.

As for magician **Andrew Oehler**, he survived war and shipwreck, but his greatest challenge was performing for the governor of Mexico. Oehler's act was so good, he was arrested and thrown in a dungeon for several months after performing. Clearly he was a sorcerer! Of course, Oehler had been *hired* to be a sorcerer, but nobody thought he'd be a REAL one. (After being released, the magician wrote his 1811 book *The Life, Adventures and Unparalleled Sufferings of Andrew Oehler*.)

For a more modern example, try visiting the Mediterranean island of Malta. You'll notice that many church towers have two clocks set with two different times. One clock is correct and the other is set to the wrong time in order to confuse the devil. (Seriously!) Or you could swing by Sweden, where a company named Häxriket i Norden announced in 2008 that it had hired twenty professional

## A Candy Bar Got Me into College

High school seniors in Japan buy Kit Kat candy bars in huge quantities. That's because it is pronounced *kitto katto* in Japanese, which sounds a lot like *kitto katsu*—"win without fail." The belief is that the candy-charmed name can improve college entry test scores. (Failing that, they also taste pretty good.)

witches to give financial counseling to people hit by the economic downturn. What good is a witch? They have skills in contacting financial consultants from the "other side"!

If you're still feeling superior to anyone who'd believe such nonsense, push the button for the thirteenth floor the next time you're in an elevator. Gotcha! You can't do it. Most buildings have floors numbered 11, 12, 14, 15, and so on. They skip 13. Why? Because nobody wants to be on the unlucky floor! (Of course, the four-teenth floor really *is* the thirteenth floor, but never mind that.) Many airplanes do the same with their seat rows—they're numbered 11, 12, 14, and so on.

But thirteen isn't the only number people have superstitions about. In China, Japan, and Korea, the number 4 is bad luck, and so *it's* the number not used in tall build-ings or plane seats. That's because the word "four" sounds sort of like the word "death" in the spoken languages of those countries. (Numbers with fours in them, like 14 and 24, are also left out). But

## Fear of Numbers

You probably already know that the fear of the number 13 is called *triskaidekaphobia*. Come-dian Graham Chapman (of Monty Python) didn't have this phobia. In fact, Graham arranged to be buried on the thirteenth hour of Friday the 13th, on the thirteenth month of the year. (Wait, just the first two.)

"eight" sounds just like the word "lucky" in Chinese, and "thirteen" sounds like "must succeed," so those two numbers are often very popular.

## NAME THAT MAGIC WIELDER!

Sometimes it can get a little confusing for an apprentice conjurer to figure out what to put on his or her business card. What is the precise word that you're looking for? Submitted for your approval are these excellent choices.

### MAGICIANS (USING MAGIC FOR ENTERTAINMENT)
illusionist, prestidigitator, sleight-of-hand artist, swindler, conjuror

*Cosmopolitan*: escamoteur

*Old School*: thaumaturge

*Very Old School:* tregetour

*Ancient School:* acetabularii

## WITCHES, WIZARDS, AND WARLOCKS
sorcerer, sorceress, enchanter, enchantress, necromancer, mage, archmage, spellbinder, witch doctor, invoker, summoner

*Neo-Scientific*: alchemist, transmuter, neuromancer (wizard with computers)

*Black Magic Practitioner*: diabolist, Satanist, voodoo poopoo-head

*White Magic Practitioner*: theurgist

## RELIGIOUS OVERTONES
shaman, fakir, miracle worker, magus

## FORTUNE-TELLERS
charmer, diviner, exorciser, medium, occultist, scryer, seer, soothsayer

113

# The First Family of Magic

*"WE ALL COME INTO THE WORLD NOT HAVING
A CLUE AS TO HOW ANY OF IT WORKS. MAGIC
RESTORES US TO THAT CONDITION."*
—John Updike

The image of a devilish-looking magician with a goatee and wearing a cape was created by the "first family" of magicians, the Herrmanns. In addition to creating an expectation of what a magician looks like, they also helped define what a magician was. **Carl Herrmann (1816–1887)** was the son of a German doctor and magician. He took his show on the road in 1847 and went to the United States in 1861. Known as "the First Professor of Magic in the World," Carl was a master of card tricks and close-up magic. But his sense of humor and entertaining manner allowed him to pull off these illusions in large theaters.

Carl's younger brother, **Alexander (1844–1896),** wasn't a bad magician either. His father had plans for him to be a doctor, but when Alexander was ten, Carl was in need of a last-minute assistant for a levitation illusion. According to Alexander, his older brother "kidnapped" him for the show, and the boy never looked back. He went solo at the age of fifteen. (No, that's not a misprint.) One of Alexander's first shows was a private showing for Queen Isabella II of Spain!

Knowing this, it comes as no surprise that Alexander became known as Herrmann the Great. When it came to showmanship, he had no equal. Alexander once plucked a watch from President Ulysses S. Grant's beard. He traveled in his own railway car and, upon arriving in a town, rode a *chariot* to the theater where he was performing! While other magicians did the Bullet Catch with a single gun, Alexander's version had *five* marksmen fire at him at once.

Alexander was a talented pickpocket who insisted that while he always returned stolen items, there was one exception: the heart of the woman who loved him. In 1875, Alexander married a dancer named **Adelaide Scarcez**

(1853–1932). Adelaide became an important part of Alexander's act; her cremation onstage was one of his best illusions. And so it was personally and professionally tragic when the Herrmanns were on an 1896 rail tour and Alexander died.

Adelaide chose to continue performing magic. After a short partnership with Alexander's nephew, Leon Herrmann, she performed her own solo act as "the Queen of Magic." She even re-created Alexander's Bullet Catch trick! Adelaide was the first major female magician, and the Queen of Magic had a long reign: she kept performing until she was seventy-five!

# *Mental Magic*

*"IS NOT THIS WHOLE WORLD
AN ILLUSION? AND YET
IT FOOLS EVERYBODY."*
—Angela Carter

As you will soon learn, reading someone's thoughts is easy. Predicting the
future? It's a snap! While you may need
simple items like a deck of cards or a live
cobra for these illusions, most important is your ability to *pretend* to have
mental powers beyond human comprehension. (*Note*: If your mental powers
*already* exceed human comprehension,

117

proceed to the next chapter: "Fun with Rubber Bands!")

Of course, some people actually *do* have great mental powers. For example, **Thea Alba** performed as "The Woman With Ten Brains." (Talk about overkill!) Alba could write or draw using her hands, feet, and even her mouth...all at the *same time*. What's more, she could simultaneously write words in different languages. Alba would even hook up a chalk-drawing device to each of her fingers, and then write ten different things on a chalkboard at once! How did Alba do this? My theory is that she really only had ONE brain, but she was quite good at using it.

Since neither you nor I is named Thea Alba (at least I'm not), we'll have to fake our amazing mental powers. In all of the following tricks, there will be a moment where you'll pretend to deduce something important or to pick up on another person's mental signals. This is what makes your magic either entertaining or ho-hum. So when you "sell" each of these tricks, be sure to lend the moment some flair or drama by concentrating really hard or asking a suspenseful question like, "Are there any wontons left?" (Or if you prefer something more honest, just say, "This will be the closest thing to actual mind reading you'll ever see.")

For instance, if you have a trick that requires mind reading, when your subject is supposed to concentrate on his or her card (or number, or whatever), close your eyes for a moment. Then look at the subject and act disappointed. "Seriously," you say, "I can't reveal the secret unless you give me access to it. Now let's try again."

*IN THE UNLIKELY EVENT THAT ONE OF THE FOLLOWING EFFECTS DOESN'T WORK, JUST SAY TO YOUR SUBJECT, "OH WELL, IT LOOKS LIKE YOUR TELEPATHIC POWERS ARE NOT FULLY DEVELOPED YET."*

Remember to dream up your own varia-tions on these tricks to make your show more authentic. Oh, one more thing. Magician Doug Henning had the ability to act as amazed at the results of his magic as the audience was. So try to seem surprised and pleased when one of your mentalist tricks works. (Speaking for myself, I *am* pleased and surprised when they do!)

## TEARING IT UP

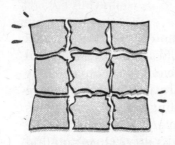

For this trick, you need a pen or pencil and any decent-sized piece of paper (square or rectangular). A paper napkin can work in a pinch. After establishing that nothing is written on the paper, tear it into nine pieces. If you're bad at tearing, fold the paper into thirds first, then tear along the folds. Finally, tear each of the thirds into three pieces.

Now, start signing pieces of the paper and casually push the CENTER piece of paper toward your subject. (It's the one that's torn on all four edges!) Have her sign it, and then combine her signed piece with your eight pieces. (If there are other people there, they can also sign any piece that isn't the center piece. Act like this will make your task harder, but that you can handle it. All this signing is good misdirection!)

Mix up the pieces and let your subject mix them too. Then, hold all the pieces behind your back. You probably won't have to fake a look of concentration, because you're feeling with your fingers along the edges of each piece of paper, looking for the one that has four rough edges! Once you find it, present it to your subject.

## PRESCIENT POINTER

For some mentalist tricks, you need an accomplice. The **Prescient Pointer** trick is one of these. You can play Prescient

Pointer with a deck of cards, but there are MANY ways you can do this same basic trick.

In addition to a deck of cards, you need anything (a pen, twig, or rigid ferret) that you can use as a pointer. Speaking to your partner, say something like, "The Spanish word *simpatico* means compatible. I feel very *simpatico* with your mental waves right now. Let's try an experiment!" Your partner agrees, and lays out nine cards face-up in three rows of three. (By the way, I'm assuming there's at least one other person around to be your audience, or you're not going to impress anyone with your mental magic!)

You explain that you will leave the room and your partner (or anyone else in the room) will silently point to one of the cards so that everyone present can see it. Then you leave the room. While you are gone, the audience member silently points out one of the nine cards to your accomplice.

Playing cards have an interior rectangle inside of them. That rectangle will serve as a layout diagram of the nine cards on the table. This is important, because when you return to the room, your partner will pick up the magic pointer and tap inside a card's rectangle while saying something like, "Is it this card?" The card he is tapping on doesn't matter. But casually pay close attention to exactly where *inside* the card's rectangle your partner taps! For instance, if your partner taps in the *middle top* of a card's rectangle, the middle-top card is the one that was "secretly" selected!

You'll know which card was selected at the very first tap, so now is when you act confused, try to pick up on brain waves, and basically create some drama. After some good acting and false starts, you'll eventually say, "I believe THIS is the card," and point to the middle-top card.

As long as your partner does the pointing, *anyone* can pick any card. But if a person also insists on being the pointer, pick up the pen or rigid ferret you've been using and shake your head sadly. Then say, "Sorry, all its magic has been used up."

## CELLULAR SENSATIONALISM

For this mind-reading illusion, you need a cell phone. You also need an accomplice with a cell phone who is not in the same room (or even the same house!) as you. You also need a piece of paper with your accomplice's phone number written on it. For this version of the trick, a deck of cards will also be handy.

Set your cell phone to "Silent." Also, if your cell phone has a "speaker phone" setting, activate it. While in private, call your accomplice—not to talk to her, but so that she can listen in on what will take place! Now situate the phone as close to your mouth as possible without it being visible (e.g., a vest pocket).

Rejoin your group and announce that you have a friend who's so good at picking up thoughts, she can read someone's mind even when not present. Now select a volunteer and have that person pick a card (any card!) from the deck. The person will show the card to the entire group, you included.

As the person does so, act like you can't see it so that the volunteer announces the card. Now clearly repeat what the card is. "So you've got the five of diamonds? Okay." Once your accomplice hears this, she will hang up. It's magic time!

Give the paper with your accomplice's phone number to the volunteer (or anyone else with a cell phone—besides you). Have your caller ring your accomplice. The caller should then repeat to the group in a loud clear voice whatever the accomplice says.

You don't have to act much anymore; just let your accomplice do a song-and-dance. "Are you thinking of the card right now? Okay, I'm getting something...It's not a

## Too Smart for His Own Good

**Washington Irving Bishop (1856–1889)** was a celebrated mind reader who collapsed after one of his performances. Doctors pronounced him dead, and hours had passed by the time Bishop's wife arrived to identify his body. The distraught woman asked that someone comb her dead husband's hair. To her horror, the comb went into Bishop's hair and then disappeared into a huge hole beneath it. It turned out that Bishop's brain was gone!

Bishop's brain-ectomy had been done during his autopsy. Either someone wanted to see a mind reader's brain or the coroner wanted to check the brain for cause of death. (The mystery was never solved.) But what the coroner didn't know was that Bishop suffered from "catalepsy." Cataleptics can pass out and *appear* dead, but actually be quite alive. (This puts them at risk for being buried alive.) So it's possible that Bishop's brain was still thinking when it was removed from his head! Weirder still, a second autopsy discovered the whereabouts of Bishop's brain. It had been put in the dead man's chest cavity. (That's not a bad pirate joke.)

Downer! Anyway, I'm sure you don't need to worry about any of that happening to you.

face card, is it? I think it might be a black card…No, strike that, it's red, isn't it? I see rings, five golden rings…wait, the rings aren't gold, but they are precious…Hey, is the card the five of diamonds?"

While the crowd "Oohs!" and "Aahs!" you might want to secretly turn your phone off to save its battery.

## DEEP POCKETS

Some mentalist tricks involve cards, but they aren't exactly card tricks. This is one of them! In order to do this trick you'll need the ability to memorize the word "CHaSeD." Note the way I capitalized it;

that's your tip to remember that, in this trick, the suits will be arranged Clubs, Hearts, Spades, Diamonds.

You need two identical decks of cards. Prepare by taking any three cards from one of the decks and putting them into one of your pockets. Lay the cards down lengthwise, with their faces facing inward. These are your "dummy cards." You're ready!

Lay the deck out face up in a wide arc on the table. Have your volunteer select any Club, Heart, Spade, and Diamond. Once these four cards are picked, fan them in the order given (with the Club's back being closest to you) and show them to the volunteer.

"Mentally pick one of these cards. Don't tell me which one!" you instruct. Then you put the four cards into your pocket...yes, the same pocket where three cards are laying lengthwise! But you put these cards in so that they rest on their short end with their faces facing inward.

You're all set. Tell the person to think of his card. As he does, look like you're concentrating and reach into your pocket to pull out one of the three dummy cards. Don't show it to your subject and don't look at it yourself, either. Just say, "It's not this one," and set it face down on the table." Keep "concentrating" and do this twice more with the next two dummy cards.

Finally, it seems as if you're down to one card. Remember "CHaSeD"? Ask your subject to now name the card he was concentrating on. As he does, you have your hand poised to go inside your pocket. If the person says "X of Clubs," you know to grab the card that is on the *outside* of the stack of cards standing on end. "X of Hearts"? Grab the card that is second from the outside. And so forth! But whatever card you do grab, make a big deal of pulling it out and enjoying his amazement!

## IT'S IN THE BAG

Many mental tricks involve you staying just *one step ahead* of your audience. This is one of them. To do it, you need at least three other people, and probably no more than twelve. You also need a small bag (or other container), a pen or pencil, and some index cards or pieces of paper.

Situate yourself with these items so that nobody can look over your shoulder at what you'll be writing. Then ask everyone in your audience to think of an important name from their lives. This could be a pet they had, an influential teacher, a bully, a famous politician...whatever! The first name that pops into their heads when you ask is the *right* name.

Say, "I'm going to write down each of the names on a card and put it in the bag." (You may wish to show them that the bag is empty now.) Now ask your audience members for the names, and to briefly explain why this name is so important. Each name will probably initiate some discussion. That's good! You want to distract people from the fact that you're actually writing down the SAME NAME over and over as you go!

In other words, say the first person reports, "I picked *ROGER KAPUTNIK*, because he gave me a piece of apple pie when I was six." As everyone mocks this person, you write "*ROGER KAPUTNIK*" on a card and put it in the bag. The next person says, "I selected our first dog *FIDO* because he taught me how to tie my shoes." You nod appreciatively and say "*FIDO*" while you write down "*ROGER KAPUTNIK*" on a card and put it into the bag. (Be sneaky! See how Fido has only four letters? Start writing, then pretend to make a spelling mistake ["Not '*Ph*ido,' duh"] and keep going.)

When everyone is done, select a volunteer. If the person is shorter than you, that's helpful but not necessary. Shake the bag and then hold it so that the person can't see into the bag. Have the person select a card with his or her eyes closed, then pull the bag away and keep it near you. Don't look anywhere near the card as the person pulls it out!

Hang onto the bag and take a step back. Ask the person to look at the card, but NOT to say anything. (You can have him or her show the name to everyone else if you want while you avert your gaze.) For drama, have the person concentrate on the card, and go through your mentalist act.

At some point, you're going to end the suspense by saying, "I believe the name on your card is *ROGER KAPUTNIK*." As everyone is suitably impressed, make a point of sticking the remaining cards in one of your pockets before someone asks to look at them!

## WHILE YOU HAVE A BAG

Another cool trick can be done with a lunch bag. Look at the side of the bag where the bottom folds up against the body of the bag. You're going to cut a rectangle out of that folded part. Next, just tape down some transparent wrap around the outside edges of the bag. This will create a window into the bag. This window should NOT be visible when the bag is folded up!

You also need six small items that *feel* identical but *look* different. For example, if you have six dice and two are white, two are red, and two are green, that's perfect. The same applies

to pencils, pens, or ping-pong balls. Any six items that are the same size but look different will work. (If all else fails, just take six index cards. Cover two cards with the number "1," two with the number "2," and two with the number "3."

You're all set! For your audience, you need at least two people. That's because you need two volunteers! Stand *between* the two volunteers while holding the bag. Only one of these people is going to see a magic show. He's Person I. If there are additional audience members, have them watch from the *other* person's side (Person II).

Explain that you have three sets of identical-feeling objects. Pick up the bag (which is folded flat) and say that in a moment, you will be putting them into the bag. Because of your mental skills, you will provide a telepathic link. Person I will reach into the bag and grab any one of the items. Person II will then be able to reach in and grab that item's partner!

The only tricky part is what happens next. Everyone EXCEPT Person I will be able to see what's going on . . . so it will only seem like magic for one person! Open the bag so that the folded window side is away from Person I. For the rest of the trick, you'll need to keep it turned that way! Quickly insert the six items and start talking so that the audience doesn't give away anything to Person I. (A smile and an unseen wink can help with this.)

Ask Person I to remove an item and keep it covered. He can't look INTO the bag, but he can look at it, so tilt the top away from him a little while he reaches in. Once he has something, turn your whole body away from Person I and toward Person II.

Tell Person I to look at his item and think of it while keeping it concealed. Then tell Person II, "Focus your thoughts and let them guide your fingers to the right item." By tilting the top of the bag away from Person II, you will only make it that much easier for her to see through the window and grab the right item!

Once she does, step back a little (while keeping the bag turned the same way) and have Person I show his item. Person II can do likewise. Repeat the trick, keeping the same Person I. You can bring in new Person IIs if you like. Don't do the trick more than four times to the same Person I. (At this point, Person I is starting to wonder what the heck is going on!) Afterward, let Person I in on the secret, and be sure to thank him for being a good sport. Heck, let him keep one of the index cards as a souvenir!

## MIND READING GIVES ME A BIG APPETITE

The idea for this restaurant trick came from Aye Jaye and Caleb and David Sohigian. It will cost you between $1 to $5, but that's a small price to pay!

Take a deck of cards. Insert into its case

## Read *this!*

**Joseph Dunninger (1892–1975)** was the most famous "mental magician" of the mid-twentieth century. In addition to a very popular radio program, Dunninger had shows on the three major TV networks, where he'd engage in mind-reading tricks. But Dunninger lost important style points because he actually claimed he had ESP.

Dunninger's claims infuriated an amateur magician named Richard Himber so much that he went to a Dunninger performance and started heckling the mental magician, demanding that Dunninger read his mind. Dunninger retorted that he would give Himber $1,000 if he could prove he *had* a mind!

between $1 to $5 and a note. Your note will read something like,

*"THANKS FOR BEING A GOOD SPORT! PLEASE KEEP THIS NOTE AND THE TIP, THEN PICK THE THREE OF*

*SPADES OUT OF THIS DECK AND REVERSE IT IN THE DECK (SO THAT IT FACES THE OTHER WAY). FINALLY, PUT THE WHOLE DECK BACK IN THE PACK AND BRING IT BACK TO OUR TABLE WHENEVER YOU GET A CHANCE."*

Take the card case (with the deck, note, and money in it) with you to the restaurant. Explain to the waiter that you would appreciate his help. Give the deck to the waiter and ask if, when he has a moment, he would mind pulling a card from the deck, reversing it, and then putting it back in the deck. Explain that this should be done out of sight of your group so that it's clear you haven't peeked first.

After the waiter brings the deck back, you can let your companions look through the deck to see which card is reversed. (If the waiter seems like a bad actor, thank him and try to get him to leave before he gives the trick away!) Finally, ask them to let you concentrate, do your act, and identify the three of spades!

This trick can be done many ways. For example, here's one that doesn't require cards. If you have a flip cell phone, ask your waiter if he'd help you with a magic trick. Hand him your closed cell phone. It already has the money and the note in it. In front of everyone, jot down the cell phone number of someone in your group and say, "Please dial this number and give the person any number between 1 and 100."

What the other people don't know is that inside of your closed phone is a note with the money and the number you want the waiter to say. After the waiter leaves, someone in the group should get a call wherein the waiter hopefully says the number you provided him. You then magically "predict" the number ("Wow, 17.4 is so specific!") and everyone is so amazed, they buy you dessert.

*NOTE:* Don't forget to get your phone back!

# Penn & Teller

*RÉSUMÉ:* Penn & Teller make fun of magicians and go out of their way to explain that their act doesn't include "a greasy guy in a tux with a lot of birds." So what are they, then? Their act has been billed as a magic show for people who hate magic. But closer to the truth is what Penn said: "We're a couple of eccentric guys who've learned to do a few cool things."

Penn Jillette started in showbiz as a tall (six foot six), fast-talking graduate from the Barnum & Bailey Clown College who became a well-known street juggler on the East Coast. Meanwhile, Teller—who goes by one name—taught high school Latin and performed as a silent magician who resembled a sly Harpo Marx. The two were a perfect match when they teamed up in 1975, and they concocted an act that could combine fire breathing, escape-artist stunts (with straitjackets and spikes), comedy, amazing stunts, and some material that can't be classified as anything BUT magic.

**TRADEMARK ILLUSIONS:** Penn & Teller don't do "illusions" or "effects." Instead they are known as "cons" and "swindles." For example, they do a Cup and Balls routine with *transparent* glasses. But they are so good at it, it's more impressive because you still can't believe your eyes!

**FUN FACT:** Penn & Teller's understanding of magic and their ability to relate to audiences has also garnered serious academic attention. They serve as Visiting Scholars at MIT, that school's highest honor, and have lectured at Oxford University and the Smithsonian Institution.

*QUOTABLE:* "All I care about are my hair and my fingernails. Everything else is just affectation." Penn Jillette

*LINT FROM DOWN UNDER:* Here's a Penn & Teller stunt that's easy to do but hard to pull off. (You'll see what I mean in a moment.) Get some thread that is a different color from the T-shirt, blazer, or Mao jacket that you are planning to wear. Thread it through the eye of a needle. Now run the needle inside the garment and poke it up through its shoulder. With the thread hanging down, cut the thread so that it's long enough to go to your waist. Pull enough of the thread through the hole so that as you put the garment on, it doesn't get pulled back inside.

Now, adjust the thread so a little hangs outside on the shoulder. It looks like lint! At some point, someone will try to pull if off, which will only pull more thread out. This gives you a chance to hop around while crying out, "Blimey, you've unraveled my underwear!"

## THE BEST MENTAL MAGIC TRICK IN THE HISTORY OF THE WORLD

I love this trick because it requires no partner and almost no sleight of hand. It's so simple, I keep thinking someone will spot the fakery, but it's worked for me every time. And best of all, it has a great payoff.

Master entertainers Penn & Teller came up with this version. While it can be played anywhere, I'll describe it as if you were performing in your home. Here's the setup: Get a deck of cards. Pull any card from the deck, say the Three of Clubs. Set this card aside. Now get a Post-It or note card. Write on it something like, "The card in the envelope is the Three of Clubs."

143

Hide or post this note anywhere you want. It can be in another room, on another floor, or outside your house. It can be miles away. *It's up to you.* Just put the note someplace where it will be undisturbed until the end of the trick.

Now, think about where the envelopes are in your house. Get a pen, pick up the three of clubs, and take the pen and card to the envelopes. Set the pen next to the envelopes. Now slide the card *face down* under the *middle portion* of the top envelope. You should be able to easily pick up the envelope, concealing the card underneath it. Practice doing this.

When you're ready for the trick, hand the deck of cards to a person and step back. It would be best if the person shuffled close to where the envelopes are. Anyway, say, "Please glance through this deck to confirm that the cards aren't in any particular order. Then shuffle the deck to your heart's content." Watch the person to

make sure that as he or she is finishing
the shuffle, the top card on the deck is
not visible.

When the shuffling is completely done,
ask the person to push the deck a little
bit away from him or herself. Say something like, "In a moment, you will take a
card from the deck. First, I have to get a
security envelope." While you're saying
this, you are getting the envelope (being
careful to conceal the card underneath
it!) and pen from the drawer.

With one hand, reach out with the pen
and say, "What time is it now?" As you say
this, you are setting the envelope with
the concealed three of clubs on top of the
deck! "Use this pen to write the time on
the envelope," you say.

The trick is basically done! Have the
person take the envelope and write the
time on it. Then have him carefully,
*without looking*, put the top card of the

deck into the envelope. Next, have the person seal the envelope and sign his name across the seal. (This is all just for effect, of course.) If you want to make the person nervous, take the envelope and put it in your pocket. Or the person can hold onto it. Either way, now lead the person to where you've hidden the Post-It note. Have the person read the note, and then open the envelope.

Although I'm writing this quite matter of factly, this is the payoff! Even if your subject is a cool customer, he or she will be truly amazed. Strike up the band! And enjoy the knowledge that you have played the Best Mental Magic Trick in the History of the World. (And if you happen to be in Southern California when you perform this, you can take your volunteer to the Forest Lawn Memorial Park in the Hollywood Hills. There, north of the Old North Church, Penn & Teller have put in a marker (called a *cenotaph*) with a picture of a Three of Clubs. At the bottom, it reads, "Is this your card?"

## Twisted Twist

Concealing a card and then placing it on top of a shuffled deck is too good a trick to use just once! Magician Max Maven did a version where he'd set aside the Four of Spades and then write a poem on a sheet of paper:

*AND SO OUR LITTLE GAME IS DONE*
*THE CARDS ARE PLAYED, THE PRIZE IS WON*
*MY FOUR OF SPADES BELONGS TO THEE*
*IN TURN THY SOUL BELONGS TO ME.*

The catch was that the poem was on a folded piece of paper with the Four of Spades beneath it. After the deck was shuffled, the magician would identify the paper as a "prediction," setting it on the deck and handing the volunteer a pencil. The volunteer would sign the bottom of the folded paper, the card would be revealed, and the poem would now be shown as a signed contract! In case you don't want to be responsible for your volunteer's soul, you may choose to come up with a different poem.

# Fortune-Telling

> "LAST NIGHT I STAYED UP LATE PLAYING POKER WITH TAROT CARDS. I GOT A FULL HOUSE AND FOUR PEOPLE DIED." —Steven Wright

The world is full of surprises, both pleasant and horrible. Why, at any point you might unexpectedly lose your house keys...or *find* mine. (Where *are* they?) How can we prepare ourselves for life's unexpected events? Yes, I could always put my keys in the same place when I get home, thanks. But I could also turn

to one of the countless "magical" ways
we humans have invented for trying to
foresee the future.

For instance, there's an entire type of
fortune-telling devoted to looking into
reflective surfaces like crystal balls,
mirrors, and pools. Called "scrying,"
these methods supposedly reveal visions
of the past and future, and even look into
the spirit world. (Hey, if you foresaw
an overhead shot of yourself knocking
over a glass of milk, you'd be *scrying
over spilled milk*!) It's a time-honored
method; in Guatemala, ancient Mayans
stared into small crystals called *ilb'al*—
"device for seeing."

Starting in the Middle Ages, seers and
Gypsies began gazing into large polished
crystal balls, which were packed in black
silk when not in use. The most famous
crystal ball enthusiast was **John Dee
(1527–1608)**, the astrologer to Queen
Elizabeth. And if you think nobody

takes scrying seriously anymore, the current Dalai Lama was selected by a group of Buddhist monks who "discovered" his identity while looking into a Tibetan lake.

Tibet is currently part of China (what a rip-off!), and the *I Ching* (ee-jing, a.k.a., *The Book of Changes*) is China's contribution to fortune-telling. With a tradition going back thousands of years, it's probably the oldest method of fortune-telling still practiced. Confucius used his copy of the *I Ching* so much, he wore out its binding three times! Anyway, the way it works involves fifty sticks and a complex set of maneuvers. This leads one to look up a section in the *I Ching*. The book features short sayings with a high moral tone, so the user might read "Moving onward with integrity brings good fortune" or "Those opposed to righteousness meet with harm."[1]

---

1 *Good advice, but should I buy a new pair of socks or not?*

## Cuppa Tea?

If you've heard of "reading tea leaves," you know that fortune-telling can be done in the comfort of your own kitchen. I'd still have to hire a fortune-teller to read the tea leaves for me. (I stare and stare at them but can't make out any letters.)

Tea-leaf reading (or *tasseomancy*) began in China sometime during the sixth century. (No one in the West even knew what tea *was* then!) If you want to try it, make a cup of loose-leaf tea. Drink MOST of the tea, and then turn the cup around three times. Next, tip the cup upside down, turn it once more, make a wish, and blow out the candles. (Oops, wrong event!) At this point the cup is lifted up and examined. Tea leaves stuck at the cup's bottom tell of the future, chunks near the rim are today, and chunks near the handle are most important. The fortune-telling starts then, but since I never liked tea, those chunks are making me queasy.

Since the tea leaves unsettle me, maybe a fortune cookie can calm my stomach. Hey, *fortune* cookies! They were probably around in Confucius's time, right? Nah, they were invented for tourists. San Francisco's Chinatown used to be a ghetto, but in the 1930s, an effort was made to "make over" the exotic neighborhood to lure tourists. Since traditional Chinese cuisine lacks desserts, a local restaurant *invented* fortune cookies. The unlikely combination of dessert with fortune-telling worked like a charm.

There are so many different ways to tell the future, it gets confusing. Some are grisly; ancient cultures LOVED to practice "haruspicy," which involves cutting open a slaughtered animal, pulling out its guts, and "reading" what they have to say. This can get pretty specific; voodoo doctors prefer chicken entrails, and in Scotland, a sheep's shoulder blade was used. (Seriously. It was called "scapulimancy.") Strangest of all may have been Peru's Incas. They would kill a white

## *What About Reading _Books_?*

The Greek suffix *-mancer* can designate a person who divines the future. Put a different root in front of *-mancer* and you've got a fortune-teller!

*Arithmancer:* A person who uses names, letters, and numbers to see the future

*Astragalomancer:* Dice reader

*Cartomancer:* A person who reads cards

*Chiromancer:* Palm reader

*Crystallomancer:* Crystal ball reader

*Geomancer:* Person who foretells the future based on marks drawn on soil or sand

*Oneiromancer:* Dream interpreter

*Padomancer:* Person who reads the soles of feet

*Tasseomancer:* Person who reads tea leaves

llama and then blow up (inflate, not detonate!) its lungs. Then the fortune-teller would "read" the vein patterns. *Blech*. More fortune cookies, please!

But if you think that's bad, this is worse. There is a field called "rumpology" in which a person's butt is "read" to determine his or her personality or fortune. Cheeky!

In a more civilized vein, a man named Al Carter was an inventor who got an idea for a fortune-telling device in the 1940s.

## Space Out and Zero In

Sibylla was a prophetess of ancient Greece. She inspired the creation of "sibyls"— women who could go into a trance and predict wars, weather patterns, and other future events. Now you know where Professor Sibyll Trelawney of the Harry Potter books got her name. (And you also know what J. K. Rowling thinks about fortune-tellers!)

First, he made a big hollow ball with a plastic window. Then he filled it with liquid. And just before he sealed the ball, he stuck a plastic icosahedron inside with fortunes written all over it. (You know what a icosahedron is, right? Right!)

Yep, he'd made a Magic 8-Ball. Is shaking this ball and reading its message just as good as any other fortune-telling device? As the 8-Ball would say, "Signs point to yes." One of Carter's challenges was figuring out what kind of liquid to put inside the ball. It needed to be something that wouldn't freeze. After experiments with molasses and antifreeze, the modern Magic 8-Ball now has a mysterious blue filling.

Cards play such a huge role in magic that tarot cards need their own shout-out. Tarot cards began as playing cards in northern Italy during the early Renaissance. Gypsies began using the tarot to tell fortunes, and the cards became widely popular for this purpose by the seventeenth century.

The seventy-eight tarot cards symbolize various virtues, vices, forces, and characters. If you've seen them before, you know there is something disturbingly cool about the dark mysteries hinted at by their artwork. For example, one card shows a tower struck by lightning, and another shows a man hanging by his feet. These are not your average playing cards!

The way a tarot reading usually works is that the fortune-seeking customer

## Psychic? Prove It

Magician James ("the Amazing") Randi has made it his life's work to investigate and expose phony mentalists and psychics who make paranormal or psychic claims. For decades, Randi has offered one million dollars to *anyone* who can show genuine evidence of supernatural powers or events. The prize still goes unclaimed.

shuffles up, pays money, and then shuffles and cuts the tarot deck. The fortune-teller then takes cards that are either dealt off the deck or selected randomly by the customer. These cards are laid out in a pattern, and an interpretation of the future follows.

In case you don't have a tarot deck or crystal ball handy, let's look at fortune-telling using a resource you do have at hand: your hands!

*PALMISTRY,* or palm reading, is the belief that your hands can reveal certain aspects of your destiny. Why would the lines on your hands have anything to do with the future? It's just a superstition! And part of this superstition is the belief that the crease to the side of the thumb in the left hand is the "life line," or what the French call *la ligne de vie.* If this line is long, that means a *long life.* If it has other lines across it, that means *sickness.* And if it is a strong line, that shows you are *energetic.* (If you don't have a *ligne*

157

> ## You're in Good Hands
>
> *MADAME ARGENTINA:* Would you like your palms read?
>
> *BUBBLES:* Oh, no thanks. I like them the color they are.
>
> —*The Powerpuff Girls*

*de vie* at all, that means you don't exist. So stop faking it!)

# THE MYSTERIES OF THE HAND REVEALED!

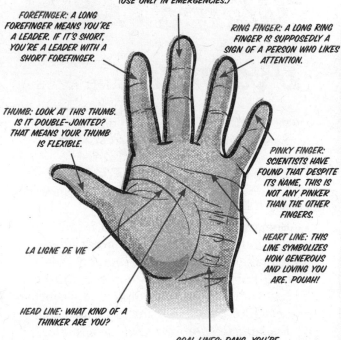

MIDDLE FINGER: THE FINGER THAT MUST NOT BE NAMED. (USE ONLY IN EMERGENCIES.)

FOREFINGER: A LONG FOREFINGER MEANS YOU'RE A LEADER. IF IT'S SHORT, YOU'RE A LEADER WITH A SHORT FOREFINGER.

RING FINGER: A LONG RING FINGER IS SUPPOSEDLY A SIGN OF A PERSON WHO LIKES ATTENTION.

THUMB: LOOK AT THIS THUMB. IS IT DOUBLE-JOINTED? THAT MEANS YOUR THUMB IS FLEXIBLE.

PINKY FINGER: SCIENTISTS HAVE FOUND THAT DESPITE ITS NAME, THIS IS NOT ANY PINKER THAN THE OTHER FINGERS.

LA LIGNE DE VIE

HEART LINE: THIS LINE SYMBOLIZES HOW GENEROUS AND LOVING YOU ARE. POUAH!

HEAD LINE: WHAT KIND OF A THINKER ARE YOU?

GOAL LINES: DANG, YOU'RE ATHLETIC!

# Weird Names AND ACTS

Because there are a limited number of illusions, magicians go to great lengths to make themselves and their acts sound original. That's why some conjurors have advertised their ability to perform acts like *Operation Paligenesia* or the *Enchanted Sciatorium*. And some outlandishly invented names stuck. For instance, French conjurer **Jules de Rovère** came up with the word "prestidigitation" ("nimble fingers") to describe the tricks he could do with cards and balls. The word took on a life of its own and can now even be found in non-magical dictionaries.

Magicians are also notorious for giving themselves grandiose stage names. Are these performers hopelessly deluded? Maybe! As **James Thompson**, a.k.a. the **Great Tomsoni,** says, "I am the Great Tomsoni, but you can call me Great." And British escape artist **Alan Rabinowitz** changed his name to **Alan Alan.** (That actually *is* sort of catchy.) What follows are some of the oddest names and acts known to magical mankind.

## Presto with the Besto

A New York writer once gushed that magician Carl Herrmann (see page 114) "prestidigitated with such dexterity and so many prestidigitorial graces, that we all fell in love with prestidigitation."

161

**Eliaser Bamberg (1760–1833)** was a Dutch magician who lost his leg in an accident. Bamberg's replacement leg was made of wood, and he had it customized with secret compartments. This allowed him to perform illusions that earned him the nickname "The Crippled Devil."

**Ali Bongo (1929–present)** was the stage name of William Wallace. As you can guess, he was going for a Middle Eastern theme. One of his most famous acts was called "Shriek of Araby," and Bongo's trademark magical phrase was, *"Hocus Pocus, Fishbones Chokus."* Unrelated to Bongo was **Hadji Ali**, the only Arabian regurgitator I've ever heard of. Performing in the 1920s, Ali's specialty was spouting gasoline from his mouth onto a wooden play structure across the stage. The structure was then set ablaze, requiring Ali to spout water and extinguish the fire.

**Kalanag** was the stage name of German illusionist **Helmut Schreiber (1893–1963)**.

As a famous performer in Nazi Germany, Schreiber found himself conjuring for Adolf Hitler more than once. "How much money do you have in your wallet?" Kalanag once asked the dictator. When Hitler responded that he never carried a wallet, Kalanag instructed him to check the pocket of his uniform. Hitler did and found to his surprise a wallet with a sizable amount of cash in it. Hitler liked that.

**Jacob Meyer** was a magician in the 1700s who knew that an unusual stage name would attract comment. So he chose **Philadelphia.** He specialized in decapitation tricks, just like real people from Philadelphia! These parts of Philadelphia's performances were so scary, they were banned in some of the countries he toured. Despite (or because of) this, he was perhaps the first internationally famous American magician. After seeing Philadelphia perform, the German writer Goethe wrote *Faust*, a story about a scholar who seeks magical power.

**Walrod Bodie, M.D. (1869–1939)** was a fake "doctor" of magic who used pseudo-science in his act. When real medical professionals objected to his use of "M.D.," Bodie explained that the initials stood for "Merry Devil." And English magician **Robert Heller (1826–1878)** already had a pretty catchy name, so he used it to his advantage: his posters read, "*GO TO HELLer's!*" And although this list hasn't been alphabetical, let's have magician **Arthur Zorka** end the stage name section. Zorka was known as **The Wizard of Awes.**

Magicians have come up with some mad monikers for their stage acts, as well. **John Nevil Maskelyne** did an act called the *Enchanted Gorilla Den*, and he built what seemed to be an automated man named Psycho who could do card tricks. **Houdini** did something called the *Crazy Crib Escape*, but that was child's play compared to his *Iron Maiden Torture Chest*. And for sheer weirdness, nobody can ever beat **P. T. Selbit**'s illusion known as *Wrestling Cheese*. From the stage, Selbit would point to an upright wheel of cheese that he called "the strongest cheese on Earth." Volunteers were brought onstage to wrestle the cheese to the ground, but a spinning gyroscope inside of it made the task impossible.

**Carl Hertz** had a relatively normal magic act, but he employed strange ways of promoting it. In 1892, Hertz advertised in local newspapers that he needed one thousand cats. Anyone delivering a cat to his theater got cash or a free ticket to the show. After receiving hundreds of cats, Hertz fastened paper collars to them that read, "See Carl Hertz at the Opera House." Then he released all of them in downtown Sydney.

Fire-eaters and fire-handlers used to be relatively common. For example, a man named **Ivan Chabert (1792–1859)** performed as both the Fire King and the "Human Salamander." Chabert had an act in which he would be put into a large oven with two raw steaks. He would then emerge, no worse for the wear, with two COOKED steaks. Chabert was also known for setting off fireworks on his back.

**Madame Josephine Giradelli** billed herself as "The Fireproof Female from Germany." Top *that*! She specialized in frightening blacksmiths by holding red-hot iron bars and washing her hands in boiling lead. (Hey, whatever it takes to get your hands clean.)

As the popularity of fire-eaters simmered down, Spaniard **José Seville** filled the void with his act as a magician named "Frakson: The Man with 1,000 Cigarettes." What did he *do* with that many cancer sticks? He produced them, disappeared them, sent sparks from the ends of them, and sometimes even (*nooo!*) smoked them.

## Why Be Yourself?

If you'd prefer to perform under a name with more showbiz than your own, try using this handy chart! (And if you have a group act, you should know that the Magnificent Magnificos is already taken.)

| Honorific | First Name | Last Name |
|---|---|---|
| Count/Countess | Rasputin | Mysterioso |
| Doctor | Druidico | Agrippa |
| Mistress | Circe | Fumidore |
| Baron | Hermes | Mallefictum |
| M.C. | Blaise | Pretendo |
| Sir | Medea | Blackstone |
| Guv'nor | Gandalfo | Faustus |
| Vecjay | Hecate | Poodini |
| Colonel | Fernando | Merlinimont |
| Madame | Charlotte-Ann | Fauntleroy |

# *Card Magic*

First, let me say that there are *thousands* of different card tricks. The key isn't in learning them all, but in picking really good tricks that you practice and can do well. Second, remember what that famous magician Mary Poppins said: "A spoonful of patter helps the magic trick go down."

So if you have a trick where you are trying to find a card, pretend to weigh each card in your hand as you go through the deck because "every time a person touches a card, it gets a little heavier." When you get to the right card, go *past* it, then return to it and say, "This seems a little heavy. Is this *your* card?"

You could also pretend you are scanning for the person's fingerprints on each card, or that you can spot the person's card by watching their reaction to each card.

## GOOD PROPS TO HAVE ON HAND

If you have ever seen something that looks like an oversized mouse pad, it was probably a "close-up mat." The sponginess of this mat makes it a perfect surface on which to do card tricks. A tablecloth with a felt-like surface can also work well.

## WORDS: HANDY THINGS, AREN'T THEY?

In this chapter, I'm assuming that you

have a traditional deck of playing cards. A "deck" contains 52 cards. A "pack" or "packet" of cards is a group of cards that you have removed from the deck. The "side" of a deck of cards is the long edge. An "end" on a deck of cards is the short edge.

What else? Your forefinger is your index finger, the one right next to your thumb. Your big finger is also known as the middle finger. (Don't point with it.) And you already know the ring finger and pinkie. Please set this book down and review your fingers now. And before you pick it up, could you make me some toast? No? Fine. Let's start.

## HIDDEN HEART

This is the easiest trick ever. First, take the four aces out of a deck. Then remove the Ace of Diamonds and put it in your pocket. You're ready!

Take the three other aces and arrange them as the picture shows. Before you display them to your volunteer, make sure the Aces of Spades and Clubs are "right-side-up" so that the person will *think* that's the Ace of Diamonds behind them! (Of course, it's *actually* an upside-down Ace of Hearts.) Tell your subject that you're going to lay the cards face-down and square them up. After you do so, you want your subject to pull out the card that is the Ace of Diamonds. Your subject will probably select the top

card, and he will be shocked that he was wrong. At that point you can shake your head wisely and pull the Ace of Diamonds from your pocket.

(Note: You can also flank the "fake" Ace with a Two and Three of Diamonds. This helps mislead the viewer into assuming there is a third Diamond in your hand.)

171

## MAGICAL TOUCH

This is a simple card-identification trick. Have a volunteer mix and shuffle a deck. When he is done, explain that you're going to try a trick. Then carefully lift the top card with your right hand. Use your four fingers at the card's top edge and your thumb at the bottom so that the card will be upright and facing away from you as you lift it. Keep the card turned well away from you during the trick so that no one can accuse you of peeking.

Reach over with your left forefinger and explain that by using your sense of touch, you will identify the card. As you touch the card in the middle, gently squeeze the top and bottom with the fingers of your right hand. This will cause the card to bow in toward your right palm. Why is this important? Because when the card bows, you will be able to see the lower left corner of the card, and the symbol of, say, the Three of Clubs that is there!

## GOING IN REVERSE

I like this trick because it's sneaky AND easy. Just reverse the bottom card on your deck. You're ready! Fan the deck out for your volunteer, being careful not to fan so many cards that the bottom card is revealed. Have your volunteer choose a card and tell him not to show it to you and to memorize it carefully.

While your volunteer does this, turn your back so that you cannot see the card. While turned, turn the deck of cards over and get it perfectly square, so that no edges are showing. (You could also just do this behind your back if you don't want to turn around.) When the volunteer is done, present the deck with the card formerly at the bottom now at the top. Have the volunteer push his card somewhere in the middle of the deck.

Very quickly, put the deck behind your back, pull the top card off, reverse it, and put it at the bottom (practice this beforehand), and bring the deck around. If there is a tablecloth or close-up mat you can use, spread the deck out on it. (If not, just spread the deck between your hands.) The volunteer's card is the only one face up!

## LOOK MA, NO HANDS!

There are so many tricks that end with "Is this your card?" it takes a special one to stand out from the crowd. This one does. All you need is a deck of cards and some salt. Yep, either put some salt in your right pocket (if you're right-handed) or secretly put a small pile of salt somewhere to the right of where you're seated.

Let your subject shuffle the deck of cards to his satisfaction. Then take the deck back and hold it in your left hand. Ask the person to cut the deck. Point to a random spot where you want him to set it down.

Next, tell him to then pick up the top card from the rest of the pile in your hand and look at it.

*KEY MOMENT:* While your subject does this, push your right forefinger into your pile of salt. Your finger should be *dry*; while the trick only needs a few grains of salt to work, use as much as possible.

Next, have your subject put the card back down on the stack of cards in your left hand. Take your salty finger and put it right in the middle of the back of that card. While you do so, say, "You're going to remember this card, right?" As your subject

assures you that he's not an idiot, gently wipe those grains of salt onto the back of the card!

The rest is easy. Keeping the cards in your left hand even (so the salt doesn't spill off), either one of you can replace the cut deck on top of the card your subject chose. Now is the surprising part. Carefully set the whole deck on the floor! Give the *whole* deck a small sharp push with the toe of your shoe. As the cards shift over, the one with the most "back" exposed will most likely be the card you want! (The salt you put on it caused the cards above to roll away.)

Pick up that card with a flourish (to brush away any salt grains) and show it to your amazed audience.

**Fun Trick**

Check the Queen of Spades in the deck you are using. If you look closely, she may be holding a Six of Spades in her hand. If so, pull the Queen and put her in your back pocket. Later, hand the deck to a volunteer and ask her to pull the Six of Spades out of the deck. After she does, have her put it back in the deck and shuffle it. Offer to find her card without looking. Just take the deck, put it behind your back, give a look of intense concentration, and produce the Queen of Spades. When your volunteer protests that wasn't the right card, point out that actually…it is!

## DO AS I DO

For this trick, you need two different decks of cards. Keep one deck for yourself and give the other one to your volunteer. Tell your volunteer to shuffle and mix his deck while you do the same. As your volunteer will be distracted, it will be easy for you to secretly note what the card on the bottom of your deck is. (For this example, let's say it's the Jack of Hearts. This card is what's called a "key card." It is a marker that helps you keep your place in the deck.)

Next, exchange decks with your volunteer. Reach into the middle of your deck, pull out a card, and look at it. Tell your volunteer to do the same thing and to REMEMBER the card he pulls. Then each of you put the selected cards on the tops of your decks. (Don't bother remembering the card you pulled. You're still focused on your Jack of Hearts, which is still at the bottom of your volunteer's deck.)

Now cut your deck once and have your volunteer cut his deck the same way. This puts your key card, the Jack of Hearts, on top of the card he selected! If you want, you can cut the deck one more time, as the odds are low that the two cards will be separated, although it COULD happen.

Tell your volunteer, "We will trade back our decks in a second. Then look through the deck until you find your card. Take it and place it face down on the table. But let me go first so you know I'm not peeking at your card."

Exchange decks. Look through your deck until you find the Jack of Hearts. The next card is the card your volunteer chose, and that's the one you place face down on the table. Your volunteer should find his card and do likewise. For the pay-off, say, "Now this should be interesting." Turn over the two cards; they'll be the same one!

## Bonus Twists!

*The Classic*

Knowing the bottom card on the deck is useful for many tricks. For example, shuffle a deck and, while you're doing so, note the bottom card (again, let's say it's the Jack of Hearts). Then hold the deck up and have your volunteer pull a card. The card is selected, and the volunteer memorizes it and puts it on top of the deck. Each of you then cuts the deck.

Now you take the deck and quickly start dealing face-up on the table. As soon as you deal the Jack of Hearts, you know the *next* card is the one the person picked. Lay it down and deal a few more cards, then stop. "The next card I turn over will be your card," you say confidently, your hand on the deck ready to deal the next card.

Your volunteer will think you're very foolish because he sees his card on the table. This will make him even more surprised and impressed when you reach back to the table and turn over his card...which is the one *after* the Jack of Hearts!

### The Lie Detector

This is basically the same trick, but with the added benefit of lie detecting. You only need one deck. Shuffle it and *note the bottom card*. Then have the volunteer pick a card from the middle. The volunteer memorizes the card, and, if you want, you can even have the person announce the card's identity. Either way, the card is put back on the top of the deck.

After this, make some patter and, while you do so, cut the deck twice. Say, "I'm going to hand the deck to you. Go through the deck, naming and laying face-down each card as you go. When you get to your card, just lie and say that it's a different card." What would have been a boring process of listening to cards being named is now fraught with tension as the person turns and names each card. Of course, as soon as your key card is named, you KNOW the next card is the selected card, so assuming the subject doesn't screw up and tell the truth, you can shout out dramatically, "Liar!"

## THE BLACK AND THE RED

As you can probably tell, I have a soft spot for magic where I do my preparation beforehand, and then all that's left to do is to perform the trick for a lucky someone. This is one of those tricks! (Oh, by the way, if you're going to do a few card tricks, have more than one deck of cards on hand. Or do your "fixed deck" trick first, then use that deck for the next trick.)

To prepare, go through the deck and pull the Nine of Spades, the Nine of Clubs, the Six of Diamonds, and the Six of Hearts. (I chose these cards randomly; the important thing is that two cards are black suits and two are red.) Put the cards in this order on *top* of the deck: Nine of Spades, Six of Hearts, Nine of Clubs. Now put the Six of Diamonds on the *bottom* of the deck. You're all set!

Give the deck to someone. Say, "Please follow these directions exactly. Make a small cut (around ten cards) into the deck. Then set that pack of cards FACE UP on top of the deck." Let the person do this, then add, "Instant replay. Now make a deeper cut (half of the deck is fine), and do the same thing. Set the cut part of the deck FACE UP on top of the deck."

Now take the deck and sort through from the top until you get to a card that's face down. Take the set of cards that were above it and set them aside FACE DOWN. Return to the deck and pick up the top two cards. (They will be the Nine of Spades and the Six of Hearts that you put there in the first place.) Don't say what suit they are, just say, "Let's play with these two cards, a *black* nine and a *red* six."

Take the two cards and set them on TOP of the pile of cards you set aside a moment ago. Ask your subject to now cut that pack of cards, so that the two cards are in the center.

You're almost done! Take the deck of cards and lift up the top half. Ask your subject to put the pack of cards on top of the remaining half of the pack. After he does, set your half of the cut deck on top of that. Now the two cards (the black nine and red six) really are buried in the middle of the deck!

Now you could just pull the top card and the bottom card from the deck and say, "A black nine and a red six!" (The Nine of Clubs and Six of Diamonds are right there waiting for you to do this.) But that doesn't seem very magical!

To end properly, hold the pack in your right hand with your left hand ready to grab it. Swing your right hand to your left hand and, at the same time, lightly press

with your top fingers and thumb. The deck will slide from your right hand to your left. As it does, keep lightly pressing down, and the top and bottom cards will come together in your right hand.

Now hold the two cards up in triumph and say, "Sweet! The black nine and the red six!" Hold it up to your audience for a moment, and once they get it, stick the cards in the deck and shuffle. (If you wait too long, they may notice the cards aren't the same suit!)

## MENTAL GRIDLOCK

This card trick is easy to do but tough for bystanders to figure out. This is my way of saying that seven-year-olds baffle college professors with it. So learn this trick! All it requires is that you memorize these four words: ATLAS, BIBLE, GOOSE, THIGH.

This card trick uses twenty cards. This is important because there are twenty total letters used in those four words, so there is one *letter* for each *card*. The magic of the four words is that between them, they only use ten *different* letters and those ten letters are all *perfectly paired off* within the word group.

So the two As in ATLAS pair off with each other. The T in ATLAS has a pair with the T in THIGH. The L in ATLAS pairs off with the L in BIBLE. And so forth!

Have your volunteer shuffle the deck, cut the deck, and otherwise prove that the deck hasn't been prearranged. Then deal twenty cards out in ten pairs, face down. Have your volunteer pick a pair while your back is turned. They memorize the two cards (make sure they're memorized!) and put them back.

You open your eyes and collect the pairs in any order, keeping the pairs together as you do so. Now in your mind, picture a grid of letters based on the four magic words.

*A T L A S*
*B I B L E*
*G O O S E*
*T H I G H*

Now keep the grid in mind! (You'll get better at it with practice.) You'll start to deal out the cards face-up. You will put each pair of cards where the pair of letters would be on your imaginary grid. Starting with A, the first card in your imaginary grid goes in the top left corner. Then you silently count out T and L, leaving space for those letters, and put the second card where the second A would be in ATLAS.

For the next pair of cards, put the first

one where the T would be in ATLAS. Now
its pair will be further down the imaginary grid. That is, it will be the first letter
of where THIGH will form. So leave some
space for the other two rows and put
that card where the T for THIGH is in
the grid.

This takes a little practice, but as long
as you remember your four key words,
you can always figure it out as you go.
Continue laying down pairs of cards on
the imaginary letters and remember that
*each letter only gets one card placed on it*.
Continuing the game, the card that goes
on the L in ATLAS will have its mate go
where the L in BIBLE is.

When the grid is filled in correctly, you're
done! Ask your volunteer to point to the
two horizontal rows in which their cards
are. *Not at the cards*, just the row. By
"reading" the two words on these rows,
you can find the two cards. For example,
if your person selects ATLAS and GOOSE,
the pair of cards has to be the cards in

the S position. The magic here is that there is always only one option. What if the person only points to one row, for example, BIBLE? Then you know it has to be the cards in the B slots.

When you get good at this, it will seem as if you're just randomly placing the cards down. This is especially true if you get good enough to go out of order; in other words, you could start with the two Os in GOOSE if you wanted to. It doesn't matter, as long as you fill in the whole grid!

## THE MAGIC WINDOW

The first time I saw this trick, I couldn't believe it. A magician had a volunteer remember a card. Then he put the card back in the middle of the deck and threw the deck at a nearby window. The card stuck on the OTHER side of the window!

To perform this takes a *little* bit of skill, but it's much simpler than you would think. First, you need two identical decks of cards. Now, pick a card! Let's say it's the Seven of Clubs. Take the Seven of Clubs from one deck and put that deck away. (Yep, you just need that one card.)

Now, you need to find a suitable window to stick the card to. This should obviously be in the area where you're going to perform the trick! Using a bit of tape or a dab of "magician's wax,"[1] adhere the card to the outside of the window. To conceal the card from the inside, you can plan on having your volunteer and audience with their backs to it the whole time you perform, but it would be easier to just partially draw the curtains to cover it.

Now, find the Seven of Clubs in the second deck, and put it at the bottom. When you're ready to perform, simply take this deck and do a *false shuffle*. The easiest way to do this is to hold the deck face down and upright in your left hand. Using your right thumb and middle finger,

---

1  *This is a soft wax for sticking stuff to stuff.*

pull a group of cards out of the middle of the pack and put it on the top. Now keep doing this process moderately quickly, so

## Magic: The Gathering

It's a card game. It's about magic. And that's all I can say. The problem with talking about Magic: The Gathering is that you need to have played the game for any comment about it to make sense. Simply put, when players get together, one of them will "rule" the others. Who that ruler will be is dictated by what cards are played. And there are a LOT of different cards.

Ah, but there is that silly title! My research shows that before the cards were released in 1993, two other names considered for them were:

*Magic:* Just Hanging Out

*Magic:* Two Decks, Two Brains, and a Shortage of Self-Esteem that you're re-ordering the cards *without changing the bottom card!*

You can ask your volunteer to tell you when to stop shuffling. When the person says, "Stop," do so, and cover the deck with your right hand. (This will seem suspicious, even though you're not doing anything!) Concentrate, then hit the deck with your hand and hold up the deck so that the bottom card faces the volunteer. (This will be the Seven of Clubs.)

"Remember that card!" you command. Then have the volunteer cut the deck, so that everyone can tell the Seven of Clubs is now in the middle of the deck. Reclaim the deck and now throw it (gently) at the window! Dramatically raise the blind (revealing the Seven) and ask the age-old question: "Is that your card?"

*NOTE:* If you'd rather not play 52-Card Pick-Up (and risk having the original Seven of Clubs turn face-up on the floor), put the deck in its box before throwing it.

# Ricky Jay

*RÉSUMÉ:* Ricky Jay might be the greatest living card performer. How good is he? It's child's play for Jay to boomerang a card around a theater, and as it flies back to him, he can cut it in half with a pair of scissors.

But in addition to being a virtuoso with a deck of cards, Jay is also a dedicated scholar of the performing arts. He probably knows more about conjuring than any of his contemporaries, and Jay writes about his more unusual discoveries in books like *Learned Pigs & Fireproof Women*. (This earned him the nickname "The Wizard of Odd.") A highly intelligent man, Jay has no interest in doing glitzy Vegas shows or cheesy TV specials.

*TRADEMARK SKILL:* Jay can throw a playing card at 90 mph. At that speed, it can cut a banana or sink into a watermelon rind.

**_EARLY YEARS:_** Ask Jay about his childhood and he'll say, "I grew up like Athena—covered with playing cards instead of armor—and, at the age of seven, materialized on a TV show, doing magic." The second part of that is true; Jay was the youngest magician ever to appear in television. ("I was awful," he adds.)

**_QUOTABLE:_** Jay is so deeply interested in storytelling and the craft of magic, he's one of the few people who can say, "I don't do tricks. I do theatrical pieces," without sounding pretentious.

**_FUN FACTS:_** Jay developed an act for Steve Martin known as the Great Flydini. Martin appeared onstage dressed in a tuxedo. Then he politely unzipped his pants and gave an uncomfortable smile as different items emerged: eggs, a lit cigarette, a ringing telephone, a glass of wine, and soap bubbles.

# Battle OF THE Magicians!

**"TO MAKE PEOPLE DISAPPEAR, ASK THEM TO FULFILL THEIR PROMISES."**
—*Mason Cooley*

The idea of two wizards going head to head in magical combat is ridiculously cool...and old school! For example, Moses and Aaron squared off against the ancient Egyptian magicians in the book of Exodus. When Aaron threw his rod upon the ground, it turned into a snake. Good one! But then the Pharaoh's magicians did the same thing with their rods. Drat! Aaron did them one better when his serpent *ate* the magician's serpents. ("In your face—er, in my *snake!*")

**Jean Robert-Houdin (1805–1871)** was a gifted French magician who is often referred to as the first "modern" magician. Robert-Houdin intended to be a watchmaker, but as a young man, someone gave him a book of conjuring marvels. Robert-Houdin's mind was set aflame by the possibilities the volume contained. He would later look back on that accidental book as the thing that saved him from having "vegetated as a country watchmaker!"

Before Robert-Houdin, magicians were essentially street performers. But the former watchmaker was able to get out of costume and into parlors and theaters for his performances. Wealthy people came to see him perform and, suddenly, magic was a legitimate performing art, and magicians could become celebrities.

After a career in which he performed for Queen Victoria and built his own theater, Robert-Houdin was ready to retire in 1856. But Napoleon III called for an encore. France had recently occupied the North African country of Algeria. But a mystical group called the *Marabout* were urging the locals to attack the French Foreign Legion and to cut ties with France. The Marabout used "magic" like fire-walking and glass-eating to reinforce their message. One of their tricks was to hand a loaded gun to someone and encourage the person to shoot the Marabout. Assuming the person actually tried, the gun wouldn't fire. The Marabout would then take the gun back and fire it into the air to prove that it was real. (The trick was that there was a small pin in the barrel that prevented the gun from being fired until it was secretly removed!)

Robert-Houdin's mission: travel to Algeria as a magical envoy and perform for the tribal leaders to impress them with France's power. Robert-Houdin wrote that the government hoped "to prove to the Arabs that the tricks of their Marabout were mere child's play... [leading] us very naturally to show them that we are their superiors in everything, and, as for sorcerers, there are none like the French." And so France's Envoy of Magic began doing performances in Algiers.

One illusion that really impressed Algerians was the Light and Heavy Chest. This was a small wooden box that Robert-

## The Lamest Threads of All

Why do so many magicians look like they're ready for dinner on a cruise ship? Early stage magicians often dressed in Chinese costumes or long exotic robes with wizards' hats. French magician Robert-Houdin chose to dress the way that spectators normally did at his performances: in formal evening clothes, with tails, a top hat, and a white tie. This formal wear became a tradition, even though the original idea of it was to *fit in*, not stand out!

Houdin brought onstage. Setting it down, he had a strong-looking local volunteer lift it and then set the box back down. Robert-Houdin then worked his magic and made the box heavy. This time, try as he might, the burly Algerian could not lift the small box. (The fact that the box was lined with metal and positioned above a huge magnet beneath the stage floor had something to do with its heaviness!)

As a final touch, Robert-Houdin had the handle of the box wired so that he could give the confused volunteer a mild electrical shock at this moment. This caused him to either step back in amazement or run from the stage. Other members of the audience often joined the shocked volunteer later in the act when Robert-Houdin "vanished" a person. He did this so convincingly that Algerian audiences were known to sprint to the exits in surprise and terror.

The French magician also included a bullet catch in his performance, but this gave the Marabout an opening in which to catch the magician as a fraud. To do so, one Marabout purportedly followed Robert-Houdin to a village, and there he challenged the magician to catch a bullet shot from his gun. To the Marabout's surprise, the magician agreed, but with the condition that he first be allowed to "pray" for six hours to get in the right frame of mind.

The deal was struck, and Robert-Houdin spent the next six hours making a gray wax replica of the round bullets shot by the Marabout's muzzle-loading gun. When the time came, Robert-Houdin asked to inspect the gun and bullets of the Marabout. In doing so, he switched his wax bullet with the lead one! So when the locals gathered in the village square, they saw the Marabout aim and fire his gun at the Frenchman. Robert-Houdin jerked back and then straightened up. In his teeth was the real bullet from the gun . . . which had been in his mouth ever since he switched it with the wax bullet!

Was Robert-Houdin's act a French success? Well, Algeria didn't achieve independence until 1962, allowing Robert-Houdin to return home and retire with some satisfaction.

## Copycat Diplomacy

A few decades later, the British government also sent a magician to Morocco to prove that his magic was superior to the local *Marabout*.

## MAGICIAN FACE-OFF

It's possible that as your reputation spreads, you may be challenged to a Magicians' Duel by a jealous conjuror. If so, stay calm and load up your pockets with dice, cards, and coins. There will be at least one referee. And make sure that all parties know the difference between a Magicians' Duel and a Wizards' Duel.

Insist that your challenger go first. This is your prerogative as the challenged. Once your rival begins his act, follow these steps.

*1. BE SMART:* If your opponent asks for a volunteer, DON'T RAISE YOUR HAND.

*2. KEEP IT MULTICULTURAL:* Assuming that the magician has coin tricks, insist that any coins he uses be pesos, euros, zlotys, or some other form of international currency. If he asks why, look exasperated and say, "It IS the twenty-first century, you know." (This is a good catch-all response to use when someone disagrees with you.)

*3. WAND CONTROL:* If your rival pulls out a wand, shout, "He has a weapon!" Advance and wrest the wand from him. (If anyone disputes your actions, point out that watching the *Harry Potter* movies has convinced you that magic wands can be deadly.)

*4. SEDATE YOUR OPPONENT:* At this point, your opponent may be irate and out of control. To ensure that he doesn't hurt himself or someone else, read aloud from this book. Your opponent will soon be docile and potentially unconscious.

*5. ABRACADABRA:* Declare yourself the winner!

## The Magic Olympics

*BACKGROUND:* Every three years, conjurors gather from across the globe to wield mighty illusions, bestow mind-blowing deceptions, and do nifty card tricks! Yes, the Magic Olympics gives magicians across the globe a chance to experience the thrill of victory…and the agony of defeat.

*CATEGORIES:* Magicians compete in either stage magic or close-up magic. Their acts last between five and

ten minutes, and they perform for a panel of (surprise!) other magicians. Scores are given in six categories, including Magic Atmosphere, Originality, Technical Skill, and Showmanship. (Winners in each category are titled as World Champions of Magic.) If it looks like a contestant doesn't have what it takes, a red light goes on and the curtain is drawn *during* the performance! Oh, the shame.

*QUOTABLE*: "Not the red light!"

*RULES:* There are LOTS, but one of the main rules is "No stooges." That means there can't be any "plants" in the audience to help with the tricks. It's also frowned upon for magicians to "vanish" low-scoring judges.

*HELL HATH NO FURY:* You might think that magicians would make the best audience of all because they know how tough it is to be onstage…and you'd be wrong! It's not uncommon for magicians at the Olympics to be taunted or heckled during their acts, and at the 2006 Olympics in Stockholm, Sweden, there was an actual riot when an unpopular act won the gold medal in "Manipulation." Judges were cursed, ushers were spit on, and no gold coins were pulled out of anyone's ears. In short, it sucked.[1]

1 *In fairness to the rioters, the act they were protesting had performed to the Riverdance soundtrack.*

# That Voodoo THAT YOU DO

> "TOO BAD YOU CAN'T BUY A VOODOO GLOBE SO THAT YOU COULD MAKE THE EARTH SPIN REAL FAST AND FREAK EVERYBODY OUT."
> —Jack Handy

If I say "voodoo," you probably think of voodoo dolls, but in real voodoo, people hardly ever use them. Voodoo's roots are in the traditional beliefs of people living in West Africa. These beliefs include theatrical sorcery, charms, ancestor worship, and spirit possession. It goes by many names; what's *voodoo* in Benin is called *juju* in Nigeria and *gris-gris* in Guinea. No matter what you call it, it's still quite popular. In the Ivory Coast recently, two thousand students demonstrated against their principal. In addition to dealing with discipline, they believed the principal practiced voodoo. So they blocked traffic and chanted, "The principal is a witch!"

Voodoo was imported into the Caribbean and southern United States when West Africans were kidnapped into slavery. New Orleans proved to be a particularly good home for voodoo. The colorful city already had French, Spanish, and American influences, and its people were practicing a combination of Catholic and Indian customs when voodoo showed up. It was easy for voodoo's juju to join the Big Easy's jambalaya.

People still practice voodoo today even though it can get them in trouble! Take a look at this actual conversation from a court trial in which a girl was accused

## The Scottish Voodoo Play

In 1936, Orson Welles directed the first professional Shakespeare production using black actors in theater history. It's now known as the "voodoo *Macbeth*," because Welles set the play in Haiti, complete with voodoo witch doctors and lots of drums. Between the voodoo and the bad luck, Welles was just asking for trouble. *Macbeth* has generated more actors' superstitions than any other play. In fact, the play is such bad luck, you're not even allowed to say "Macbeth" in a theater. (It has to be called "the Scottish play.")

of practicing voodoo at her school. (This was against the rules. Go figure!) The girl's mother was on the witness stand to defend her.

*Q: DO YOU KNOW IF YOUR DAUGHTER HAS EVER BEEN INVOLVED IN VOODOO OR THE OCCULT?*

*A: WE BOTH DO.*

THAT VOODOO THAT YOU DO

*Q: VOODOO?*

*A: WE DO.*

*Q: YOU DO?*

*A: YES, VOODOO.*

You know what they say: The family that makes voodoo together…uh, goes to trial. Anyway, if you visit New Orleans, you will definitely notice a certain dark-haired gypsy portrayed in the local figurines, amulets, and charms that are for sale in many shops. That woman is the Voodoo Queen of New Orleans, **Marie Laveau (1794–1881)**. Marie's grave by the French Quarter is visited by about a quarter of a million people each year. Laveau's voodoo was supposedly so powerful that the Voodoo Queen's other name was "the Pope of Voodoo."[1]

Marie Laveau had a mixed heritage,

---

1 *I just used the word "voodoo" three times in one sentence. Do I get a prize?*

with black, American Indian, Spanish, and French blood. (New Orleans folks called people like this "quadroons.") After learning how to make voodoo magic and charms, she worked as a hairdresser. Marie began telling fortunes, reading palms, and providing protection from the evil spirits of the supernatural world. Using her social and business contacts, she created a network of clients. In short, she was a good businesswoman!

## Schools and Voodoo, Part II

In 1992, a substitute teacher in New Jersey enlisted the aid of voodoo to gain control of an unruly class. Monique Bazile chanted, tossed ritual powder on the students, and threatened that their homes would catch fire if they didn't behave themselves. She was charged with criminal counts that included endangering the welfare of a child.

But she was a *bad* businesswoman, too. Marie was a big woman, and she would give her rival voodoo queens a beat-down in the street to put them in their place. By the time she was in her thirties, Marie Laveau ruled New Orleans.

People were amazed at Marie's skills in knowing hidden secrets and truths. They thought she might even be a mind reader. The truth seems to be much simpler. Marie was an expert at gossip collecting. So if a servant told her the secrets of a wealthy woman, Marie could *pretend* to learn these things with voodoo. The moral of the story? Gossip is more powerful than black magic.

# Houdini

**"HOUDINI WAS A TERRIBLE MAGICIAN."** —*Jim Steinmeyer*

Here's a neat trick: **Harry Houdini (1874 –1926)**, the most daring, imaginative, mysterious showman of his age, *wasn't* Harry Houdini. He was Ehrich Weiss, a Hungarian who was seventeen when he took a stage name inspired by the famous French magician Jean Robert-Houdin (see page 195).

Houdini was a short man—only about 5 feet 5 inches—but powerfully built and

very flexible. He worked in carnivals and cheap circuses as an acrobat. While doing so, he went to museums, police stations, and locksmiths and studied hundreds of locks. First, he figured out how to pick them, and then he practiced doing so under unusual circumstances. And so the way he first gained fame was as the "Handcuff King," the man who could escape any pair of handcuffs.[1]

Padlocked chains and locked jail cells were no proof against Houdini. When Houdini visited a town, he would ask to

---

1  *I can do something nearly as impressive: I can get out of any pair of socks put on me.*

escape from its jail. After being searched for keys (and sometimes stripped), he would be locked up. Police and spectators alike would be astounded when a fully clothed Houdini would shortly join them. And after visiting an insane asylum in Nova Scotia, he added straitjacket escapes to his repertoire.

Houdini also learned that adding an element of danger made for a better show. Why just escape handcuffs when you could do it underwater? Why sneak out of a straitjacket when you could do

## What a Showman!

When waiting to appear onstage, Houdini stood several steps behind the stage curtain. When his introduction began, he would begin walking toward the curtain so that as it opened, he was already approaching the audience and taking command of the stage.

the same thing while hanging from a skyscraper fifty feet up? Accepting challenges was another way to get publicity. In 1904, when a blacksmith spent five years constructing "unpickable" shackles, Houdini agreed to be locked in them onstage at London's Hippodrome theater. Houdini had to stop three times and at one point removed a pocket knife from a pocket to cut his coat off himself. (He needed flexibility to operate.) In the end, it took over an hour, but he did it.

In 1906, Houdini had himself locked up on Murderers' Row, in the former jail cell of Charles Guiteau (the man who shot President Garfield). Not only did Houdini escape, he unlocked his fellow prisoners as well, moving them from cell to cell and confounding prison officials!

Houdini's water escapes alone were legendary. In one classic, he was handcuffed and then nailed inside a wooden crate. The crate was then submerged in a river. Onlookers would be convinced that

## Pick One!

How did Houdini get his picks? He was almost always searched carefully before stunts and sometimes was even stripped to ensure that he wasn't smuggling them. (One of his publicity posters read, "Positively the Only Conjurer in the World Who Strips Stark Naked"!) Some theories:

★ HIS WIFE, BESS, WOULD KISS HIM AND PASS THE PICK WITH HER MOUTH AFTER HE'D BEEN SEARCHED.

★ HE WOULD PLANT THE PICK IN THE LOCATION HE'D BE LOCKED INSIDE.

★ HE'D USE A MAGICIAN'S MISDIRECTION TO PALM THE PICK AND MOVE IT AROUND DURING THE SEARCH.

★ HIS HAIR WAS SO THICK AND WIRY, HE'D JUST STICK THE PICK IN THERE.

★ HE WOULD EMBED OR STICK THE PICK IN THE THICK SKIN ON THE SOLE OF HIS FOOT.

★ HE HAD A SWISS ARMY KNIFE SURGICALLY IMPLANTED IN HIS PANCREAS.

## Getting Into Show Business... Literally

**Seamus Burke (1888–unknown)** was the opposite of Houdini. That is, Burke specialized in "enterology"—getting *into* things. Burke made a name for himself by mysteriously appearing inside locked trunks and sealed bags during his performances.

the great man had died, but moments later, he would pop up.

Less water but more danger was involved in the Milk Can Escape. I know what you're thinking: Nobody can escape from a milk can except the lactose intolerant! But it turns out that Houdini could. He would crouch handcuffed inside a forty-two-inch milk can full of water while the lid was padlocked. A screen would be placed in front of the can, and a couple of minutes later, he would appear.

In London, a brewer challenged him to do the Milk Can Escape using beer instead of water. Houdini, who didn't drink alcohol, accepted. Mistake! Once he was locked in the can, the fumes from the beer overcame him, and Houdini's assistants had to knock the padlocks off with axes to save the unconscious magician.

In 1908, Houdini escaped from *inside* a burglar-proof safe. Although its door was covered with a steel plate, Houdini snuck into the safe before the performance and

### My Favorite Escape Story of All Time

Magician Harry Blackstone and Harry Houdini once drove to a magic convention. Upon arriving, Blackstone hopped out of the car, but Houdini kept struggling with his door. Finally the greatest escape artist in history called to Blackstone: "Get me out of this thing—I'm locked in!"

## *Birth of a Star*

When comedian Albert Brooks was in high school, he went to Carl Reiner's house and tried to impress the show business legend with an impression of Houdini. After being introduced, Brooks was supposed to come in from the patio to show off what a great escape artist he was. But Brooks couldn't even make it through the screen door! He eventually ran around to the front of the house to get inside. Meanwhile, Carl Reiner was laughing so hard, people worried for his health.

changed its springs. After being locked in, Houdini opened the safe in seconds. But he didn't want to be too obvious, so he goofed off for fifteen minutes before victoriously leaping out to the audience.

Four years later, Houdini unveiled what he called his most difficult escape ever: the Chinese Water Torture Cell. With his ankles locked in stocks, an upside-down Houdini was lowered into a glass-fronted, water-filled cabinet. Once he was in, a lid was padlocked in place over him. He was out in two minutes.

As an escapologist, Houdini escaped honestly, if possible. If not, he cheated! Either way, the audience almost always left entertained. But his *magic*—please. Houdini was so frustrated with his conjuring skills, he once said, "I am determined to give a good magic show before I die."

Even so, Houdini pulled off the Vanishing Elephant illusion. In 1918, he had an elephant brought onstage at a New York theater and led into a cabinet. Moments later, the cabinet was opened, and the elephant was gone. Good one! Houdini did an excellent job keeping the secret of this illusion. When asked how he did it, he'd answer, "Even the elephant doesn't know."

Houdini hated frauds, spiritualists, fortune-tellers, and mediums more than almost any magician. His friend Arthur Conan Doyle (and creator of Sherlock Holmes) believed in psychics and spiritualism. Doyle's wife was a spiritualist, and she claimed to have channeled Houdini's dead mother while writing sixteen pages of messages to him. Houdini was

## Identity Crisis

Harry Haudini was just one of the many imitators who tried to copy and rip off Houdini's act. This led Ricky Jay to consider writing a book about them titled *I Houdini: Howdini, Oudini, Martini-Szeny, and Zucchini, Pretenders to the Throne.* Of course, every successful magician had his material and name stolen. Scottish magician John Henry Anderson was known as the Wizard of the North. Once he was famous, there was a Wizard of the East, a Wizard of the West, and a Wizard of the South in no time!

convinced it was a fraud, because his channeled mother called him "Harry" while in real life she always called him "Ehrich." This led Houdini to attend séances undercover with the intent of exposing the spiritualists as fakes.

In 1926, Houdini was in Montreal being interviewed by college students when one of the students apparently asked if he could punch the magician in the stomach. This sounds odd, but Houdini was in such great shape, he sometimes let people punch him in the midsection *after* he'd tensed his abdominal muscles.

Houdini agreed to the student's request, but the magician was unprepared when the student lunged forward and punched him multiple times with great force. Houdini performed his show afterward, but he was in so much pain, he went to a doctor who diagnosed him as having acute appendicitis that was aggravated by the blows. He died some days later, on Halloween. In his will, Houdini had requested that upon his death, all the letters he'd written to his mother be gathered up and used as a pillow for him in his coffin. And so they were.

Houdini was an amazing performer and a great escape artist, and he was wildly original in the stunts he concocted. His ability to make every performance seem like a near escape from death has made countless magicians like **Criss Angel** and **James Randi** replicate his feats. In an homage to Houdini's death, **David Blaine** even had a mixed-martial arts fighter punch him twice in the stomach *really hard*. (It was pretty fakey, though. I mean, Blaine survived.)

# Delightful Effects

Believe it or not, there are some magic tricks that don't include coins, cards, hoops, saws, mirrors, or swamp gas. These tricks do, however, often involve fresh fruit. And so I present you with:

## THE CONSIDERATE BANANA

For this trick, you need a long needle (or a piece of thin, strong wire) and a banana. The trick works especially well if the banana you choose is still attached to a bunch.

Before doing this trick, take your needle and stick it into the banana body about a third of the way down from the top. Push it in until you think you've hit the skin on the other side. Then carefully shift the needle to the right and left. This will slice it inside the peel! Now do this one more time about a third of the way up from the banana's bottom. If your banana is still attached to the bunch, mark it somehow so that you can spot it later.

When you're ready to perform, your patter could be something like, "As you know, tangerines and oranges are already conveniently separated into bite-size sections. I believe that using a little magic, I can persuade bananas to be just as considerate." If you have any magic phrases or motions you'd like to use, do so. Then pick your special banana, peel it, and marvel at how considerate the banana is!

## GRAPE EXPECTATIONS

Anytime there are grapes around, you are now legally obligated to do one of these tricks. The first one is easiest. While eating some grapes, stick one into your mouth and leave it there. Then take another grape. Using silent mime skills to get attention, hold it up for all to see, then hold it with the tips of all four of your fingers and your thumb so that half of the grape is sticking out from your fingertips.

Now press your fingertips against your ear. This will push the grape out of the sight of your onlookers. Continue pushing and pressing while covering the grape with your hand. As you do so, act as if a grape is coming in from the back of your mouth. Puff your cheeks and synch the appearance of the hidden grape from your mouth with your hand motion. Ta dah!

For your second grape trick, hide a grape in your mouth again. Now get another grape and hold it with the thumb and middle finger on your right hand. Now, you are going to want to pretend to put that grape in your left hand. Do this just  like one of the coin passes mentioned in the Money Magic chapter (see page 82). If you haven't read it yet, do this:

*1. OPEN YOUR LEFT HAND.*

*2. AS YOU MOVE YOUR RIGHT HAND (WITH THE GRAPE) TOWARD IT, TURN YOUR WRIST INWARD, BLOCKING THE VIEW OF THE SPECTATORS FROM WHAT YOU'RE ABOUT TO DO.*

3. *TOUCH THE GRAPE TO YOUR LEFT PALM AND CLOSE YOUR FINGERS AROUND IT WHILE STILL KEEPING IT BETWEEN YOUR RIGHT FINGERS!*

4. *WHEN YOUR LEFT HAND'S FINGERS TOUCH THE BACK OF YOUR RIGHT HAND, MOVE YOUR RIGHT HAND AWAY (NOW GENTLY CUPPING THE GRAPE) AND DROP IT TO YOUR SIDE OR UNDER THE TABLE IF YOU'RE SEATED. LOOK INTENTLY AT YOUR LEFT HAND AND <u>PRETEND</u> THE GRAPE IS IN YOUR LEFT HAND.*

5. *SLAP YOUR LEFT HAND ON TOP OF YOUR HEAD AND SPIT OUT THE GRAPE IN YOUR MOUTH!*

## THE MAGIC Q-TIP

One thing that will give you confidence is proving that the hand really is quicker than the eye. In other words, you can outright fool a person who is watching you do a trick! To do so, you need some Scotch tape and a toothpick or Q-tip. If you're using a Q-tip, break off the end so that it's about as long as a toothpick.

Tape the end of the Q-tip to your right

thumbnail so that the length of it runs down your thumb. Now keep your thumb concealed until you're ready to do the trick. Standing directly in front of your subject, hold up your fist so that your thumbnail is concealed behind your forefinger and the Q-tip is sticking straight up. Then either snap your fingers (on your other hand) or just suddenly blow on the Q-tip. Simultaneously, open your right hand so that

## Quick Idea

Get a rubber hand that clamps onto the edges of things. Then stand behind something like a door and look around it. This establishes to anyone watching that this is your hand. (Put your face by it and smile, for example.) Then do something "magical" like entering the room with one hand in your pocket. If anyone reacts, look surprised and say, "Oops." Go back behind the door, take off the hand, and put it in a pocket, then re-emerge with both of your hands visible!

all your fingers and thumb are erect with your palm facing your audience. This will conceal the Q-tip. To your subject, the darn thing just disappeared!

Oh, and this trick is designed to fool the person standing in front of you, so don't expect it to work on anyone else.

## EXTREME BANDWIDTH

Put a rubber band around your forefinger and index finger, down by the knuckles. With your palm facing down, let the rubber band hang downward. Now curl all four fingers inward and wrap the rubber band around them. So looking at your fist from above, the

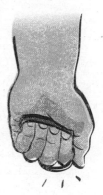

rubber band is still covering your first two fingers, but looking from below, the outer joints of all four fingers are covered by the rubber band.

Now open up your fist. The rubber band jumps over to cover your ring finger and pinky! Now do exactly the same thing you did above from this new position. It will jump back to its starting point! To make this trick more interesting, take two rubber bands of different colors. Start with one around your forefinger/ index finger and the other around your ring finger/pinkie. Wrap both around the ends of your fingers. Opening your hand will cause them to switch positions!

For the final mindblower, set up your hand with two rubber bands hanging down, as described above. Before wrapping these around all four finger joints, take a third rubber band and wrap it around just the ends of all four fingers. Now go ahead and also wrap the bands that are each around two of your fingers.

The trick will work as it did before, but it also gives you the chance for some interesting patter: "This final rubber band is for security. It makes it impossible for the other rubber bands to escape and move from one side of my hand to another." When the rubber bands DO switch, you should act as amazed as anyone!

## THAT'S LEVITATION, HOMES

If you are ever around Styrofoam cups, remember this trick. To do it, fill your cup with a beverage, like apple cider or perhaps grape juice. Drink it naturally, and when the cup is empty, *cough*. At the same time, punch a hole through the side of the cup with your thumb. Do this about a third of the way up from the cup's bottom.

This trick works best for people in front

231

of you and to one side. So if your audience is to your *right*, insert your left thumb into the cup (and vice versa if people are to your left.) Then give whatever patter you like (e.g., "Golly! Me cup is floating!") and raise the levitating cup up high. Don't do it too long, and be sure to crush and recycle the cup afterward.

## THAT'S CARBONATION, HOMES

The same trick can be done with a drink can, as long as you don't mind putting a little rubber cement (not Krazy Glue!) on yourself. Dry the side of the can you're going to drink and put a little dab of rubber cement on the side near the top. Then put a little on the end of one of your thumbs. Now you're set! Drink the can's contents—yes, the rubber cement will dry, but don't worry. Once it's empty, push your dabbed thumb against the spot of rubber cement on the can. It will stick! With your other hand, put a finger beneath the can for balance. This will now be a great trick for anyone directly in front of you, because you can now remove the bottom support. That means that for anyone directly in front of the can, it appears to be floating in air!

## THE BALDUCCI LEVITATION

**David Blaine** made the Balducci Levitation famous, although it had been around for years. You don't need a single prop for this trick. It works best in a room, especially one that's not brightly lit. Perform the levitation for one to four closely grouped spectators.

Begin by standing with your right-hand side to the group and then taking a few steps. You should be eight to ten feet away from them. Stop and stand still with your feet together (especially the heels). You should be able to look over your right shoulder and see your audience. By staying at a right angle from them, the toes of your left foot are hidden from their eyes. That's important.

Spread your arms to the sides for balance, and if you're going to engage in any patter, now's the time. (Something like, "Oh, forces of gravity and air, I beseech you to help me rise!" or maybe "Eep! I'm floating. Mommy!") As you do this, keep your right foot straight and stand up on the toes of your left foot. The audience will see the heel of your left foot and all of your right foot rise in the air. Amazing! (Note: It helps to wear pants for this, as the cuffs of your pant legs will also obscure the vision of the spectators.

Slowly rise and then hold this pose for just a few seconds. Practice beforehand so you don't lose your balance and spazz out. When you let yourself down, thank the spirits of gravity and air for their help (don't forget Mommy!) and bask in adoration.

## MAGIC MARKING

For this trick, you actually do need a black-tip magic marker. A few moments before you perform, take the marker and use it to fill in a small circle in the center of the pad of your right middle finger. Let it dry a little and reapply a couple of times so you know there is some wet ink there. (Note: If you don't want to hassle with ink, colored chalk works very well for this effect.)

Put the pen in your right pocket and, shortly thereafter, approach your volunteer. Explain that you want to show her a quick demonstration of how receptive she is to the unexpected. (This is just patter!) Being careful not to show or smudge your marked finger, ask her to hold both of her hands out palm down.

This is the part that needs to be natural. Maintain eye contact and, without looking at anyone's hands, take each of her hands in yours. As you do, explain that "they

need to be a little higher/farther apart."
As you shift her hands, apply gentle but
firm pressure with ALL of your fingertips to her palms. (Your right finger will
now leave a mark in the middle of her
left palm.)

You're done! So take your time here, as
it will help her forget when you may
have left the mark. With her hands still
sticking out, tell your volunteer to make
a fist with both hands. Then take out the
pen, holding it with your right hand so
that it conceals the dot on your finger in
the process.

Take the pen and fill in a dot in the
middle of your left palm. It should be
about the same size as the dot you made
earlier! Now let go of the pen and use
the forefinger and middle finger of your
right hand to rub the wet dot a little.
(Now your old dot is safe from discovery.)
Take your two fingers and make a magic
motion over the top of the volunteer's
closed *left* fist.

Ask the volunteer to open her fist. Voila! The black mark has magically passed through her hand and onto her palm! Now praise your volunteer and see if she has a piece of gum.

## David Blaine

**QUOTABLE:** "David Copperfield made the Statue of Liberty disappear, but then it came right back. My ideal magic would be to make the Statue of Liberty disappear so that it *never* comes back, even if I have to go to jail afterward."

**RÉSUMÉ:** David Blaine was performing card tricks at parties when he was thirteen, but he appeared on the national magic scene when he started performing in tough New York neighborhoods in the mid-1990s. A soft-spoken Puerto Rican with short hair and wearing a T-shirt, Blaine was the opposite of the glitzy white guy-with-big-hair magician as epitomized by David Copperfield. Blaine struck a chord, and he had his first *Street Magic* TV special by 1997.

As a Houdini devotee, Blaine became increasingly interested in escape artistry and physical endurance instead of magic. For one of his tricks, he would lie in a coffin, but instead of being "dead" and coming back to life, Blaine would just try to stay alive during the seven days he'd spend in a Plexiglas coffin that was underwater.

Blaine survived. And it led him down a new path of doing stunts that were part endurance test, part performance art, and sometimes lame. For example, in 2003, he did an act called Above the Below. For it, Blaine fasted for 44 days inside of a glass box in London. That's entertainment? But that was as good or better than his

Dive of Death. Bystanders booed the finale and Blaine himself called it a "disaster."

**FUN FACTS:** During his glass box fast, onlookers hurled sausages at Blaine. One person flew a remote-controlled helicopter carrying a hamburger to him to see if Blaine would eat it.

**TRADEMARK ILLUSIONS:** Blaine became popular for his *Street Magic* video footage of piercing coins with a cigarette and doing the Balducci Levitation. (Other magicians grew so jealous, two episodes of the TV show *Magic's Biggest Secrets Finally Revealed* seemed to be devoted to debunking Blaine's act.)

# Magicians

## FOR DISMEMBERMENT

Magically dismembering a person and then putting him or her back together is an illusion with a centuries-old tradition. (This raises the question "What the heck is *wrong* with these magicians?") For example, in Japan, Shinto warriors would display their courage with a decapitation trick. One warrior would kneel down while another (armed with a samurai sword) would place an apple on the back of the warrior's neck.

The swordsman would then wind up and kapow! The apple would be split in half, but the warrior was unharmed!

The key was the small iron bar inserted down the apple core. But even so, there was plenty of room for error. If the swordsman was a little off in his swing, there would be a split melon to add to the fruit bowl.

In 1584, **Reginald Scot** wrote of a trick called the "Decollation." First, the magician's assistant would lie down on a long table covered with a cloth. A plate was set under his head. Then his head was covered with a cloth. Next, the magician would take out a meat cleaver and seemingly cut off the assistant's head!

The magician then lifted the plate (still covered) and moved to the other end of the table. A small, smoky fire was started in front of the plate (necessary for camouflage), and then the cloth would be removed. Amazingly, the decapitated head would open its eyes and begin to speak!

Of course, the assistant had stuck his head through a hole in the table, while another hidden assistant poked his head up from under the table at the other end. Still, it was a good trick! Of course, the most famous variation of the "dismemberment" illusion is the version where the magician puts his assistant into a long box with his head and feet exposed. Next, the assistant is cut in half. Then he is (usually!) put back together.

Magician **P. T. Selbit (1881–1938)** is often credited with popularizing the illusion he called Sawing a Woman in Half in 1921. It was done with a handsaw; there was no blood, and the woman was always back in one piece by the end of the show. It was such a hit that Selbit followed it up with Crushing a Woman, Destroying a Girl, Stretching a Girl, and The Indestructible Girl. (No, I'm not making these up.) Other magicians quickly jumped on the fad of putting women in danger, notably **Servais Le Roy**'s Subduing a Woman With Bayonets and **Horace Goldin**'s Tearing a Woman Apart. (These acts were not nearly as bad as they sound, but still...why did people buy tickets for them?)

Other riffs on the idea of bisecting someone: Horace Goldin ramped up the illusion in noise and spectacle by being

## *A Question*

Why did women get sawed in half so much? Sure, it was a popular fad then, but maybe that's why there aren't that many female magicians today. They got sick and tired of their poor treatment onstage. (Another theory is that most adults who are interested in magic used to be KIDS who were interested in magic. So perhaps little boys like to show off more...or maybe men just have a higher geekiness factor. Dunno!)

## Look at My Thumb!

If you insist on learning a trick where someone gets dismembered, you're going to have to play all the parts. You'll need a paper napkin, a carrot, and a steak knife or some scissors. You'll do the trick seated, so smuggle the carrot (and if you're using them, the scissors) to the dinner table or into a restaurant.

Start by carefully getting the carrot out on your lap. Next, take your paper napkin and spread it over the carrot. Now it's time for patter: maybe you've lost feeling in your thumb lately, or to keep from sucking your thumb you're ready to cut it off, or about how the mind can control pain…as with almost all magic, the patter doesn't matter!

Anyway, with your left thumb sticking up, bring the napkin (with the carrot underneath) up and over your thumb. As the napkin descends, grab the carrot with your fist…it's your new thumb! (From under the napkin, nobody will be able to tell.) Now, quickly and dramatically cut your "thumb" off or have someone else do it for you. Give a horrified look at the group and cry out "The pain! Why did I do it?" or "Forget science, I'm donating my body to magic!" Then quickly hide all the evidence (napkin, carrot parts, left hand) in your lap and act like nothing happened.

the first to use a buzz saw for his performances. More recently, Peruvian magician **Aldo Richiardi Jr.** would saw his own daughter Rena in half at the end of each show. It was a grisly scene, with blood flying all over the stage. After Richiardi was done, he didn't even put her back together again! Richiardi would assure the crowd that she wasn't *really* dead, and then he would end by saying, "The real question isn't 'Was it a trick?' but 'Was it done well?' " *Ulp.*

In 1956, Indian magician **P. C. Sorcar (1913–1971)** went on British TV to perform the buzz saw illusion. Sorcar sawed his assistant (who was named Dipty Dey!) in half. Then Sorcar dipped a cleaver into Dipty to prove she really was in two pieces. And then, with no time remaining, the program ended! Scotland Yard was besieged by people reporting a murder they'd just seen, the BBC's phone switchboard was jammed by callers phoning in to see if Dipty Dey was okay, and the story was headline news the next day. (Despite her name, Dipty was fine.)

But the most shocking version of this trick ever was put on by **Johnny Eck**. After being cut in half by a magician and reassembled, Eck returned to his seat in the audience... But suddenly, he fell down, and his body split at the waist, with Eck crawling with his arms one way while his legs ran off in another direction!

Not to worry. Johnny Eck had been born without legs, so to "walk" he stood on the shoulders of a dwarf whose entire body was covered in a regular-sized pair of pants! But people were so traumatized by the shock of what they'd seen, his trick had to be (temporarily) retired.

Along the lines of gruesome magic, the Indian Rope Trick sounds innocent enough. The basic idea is that the end of a rope slowly rises in the air and remains suspended. A boy then climbs up it, but when the magician claps his hands, the rope falls to the ground and the boy has disappeared. (This trick was first recorded in 1355, when North African traveler Ibn Batuta described it.)

Another legendary version has the magician climbing the rope after the boy and both disappearing. And the Rope Trick's least family-friendly variation has the kid being caught by the magician at the top of the rope. There he is chopped into pieces, which are dropped downward into a basket by the rope's base. The magician descends alone, and out of the basket leaps the boy, magically reassembled!

But it turns out these are *all* legends. There is no such trick in any of these forms, and it's never been performed...or at least, not performed well. Rats!

The Indian Basket Trick also capitalizes on the spectator's fear that someone is being carved into pieces. It works something like this: From the audience's viewpoint, they see a person (usually small, young, and flexible) climb into a wicker basket. The magician puts a top on the basket and then takes out a mean-looking sword.

The sword is then plunged into the basket and the kid in the basket shrieks in pain. The sword comes out bloody! Again and again the sword is plunged in until all is silent. The sword is wiped clean. The magician takes the lid off the basket and tilts it to the audience. No kid! Then the magician sets the basket back down, and as he

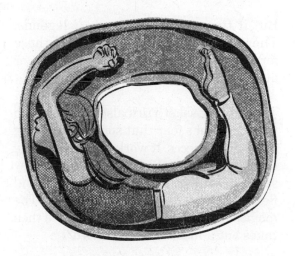

does so, the child emerges...unharmed! Oh, thank goodness.

The key to this trick is the basket's round-bodied design. It allows the child to hug the edges of the interior while the sword passes above (or below) her body. The blood? Small sacks filled with red dye do the trick. And why didn't the audience see the kid? Because of both the basket's unique design and the artful way that the magician tilts it!

# *Movie Magic*

*"THE AUDIENCE KNOWS THE TRUTH: THE WORLD IS SIMPLE. IT'S MISERABLE, SOLID ALL THE WAY THROUGH. BUT IF YOU COULD FOOL THEM, EVEN FOR A SECOND, THEN YOU CAN MAKE THEM WONDER, AND THEN YOU...GET TO SEE SOMETHING REALLY SPECIAL:...THE LOOK ON THEIR FACES."* —The Great Danton in
The Prestige

What you are about to read next will change your life forever.[1]

---

1  *The change will be so subtle, you may not notice it.*

## *Have Chores? Learn Magic!*

The 1940 Disney film *Fantasia* has a story called "The Sorcerer's Apprentice." In it, Mickey Mouse plays the part of the apprentice who learns a spell that brings lots of brooms to life so they can do chores like fetching water. But since Mickey doesn't know the spell to get the brooms to STOP bring water, chaos ensues. (Along with the cool animation, I like the fact that Mickey's adventure was based on a 2,000-year-old story by a writer named Lucian.)

Magicians were movie-making pioneers! In the late 1700s, conjurors began using early overhead projectors called "magic lanterns." A "slide" with a clear drawing was hung on the side of the lantern. When the lantern was lit, it would project the image forward, usually onto billowing smoke that the magician provided.

The lantern was hidden from public view,

so when the ghostly image of a person, angel, or demon appeared within the smoke, everyone was very impressed. These ghostly images could even change in size if the magic lantern was put on rails and moved back and forth. Not bad!

But when magician **David Devant (1868–1941)** saw something called "living pictures" in 1896, he was inspired. Devant immediately got some film equipment and shot footage of himself pulling a rabbit out of a hat. It was the world's first special effect!

David Devant sold a film projector to fellow magician Georges Méliès, the man now known as "the father of science-fiction movies." Méliès was interested in capturing magical illusions on film that could not be done onstage. He was the first to discover stop-motion animation. Using this technique, Méliès made a number of famous fantasy films that have unmistakable touches of whimsical humor. Consider the 1902 *A Trip to the*

*Moon* and its famous image of the Man in the Moon with a rocket stuck in his eye!

Méliès recognized that his movie magic was quite different from performing stage magic. As he said, "In conjuring, we work under the eye of the public. In filmmaking, we are far from public sight." Ironically, as movies grew more popular, they began to undermine the audiences that had once paid to see magicians and other live entertainers. After all, anyone with a camera and a film splicer could make someone disappear! Even so, Houdini was very interested in film. He starred in five feature movies, but audiences were already familiar with the stunts and tricks of the camera. Houdini found that the performances that got a tremendous audience response live just didn't work onscreen.

This redirected some magicians into working on sleight-of-hand instead of

## One Last Trick Before I Go

Orson Welles wrote, directed, and starred in what is usually considered the greatest movie of all time: the 1941 *Citizen Kane*. Welles was also very interested in magic. As a guest host on *The Tonight Show*, Welles skipped the opening monologue and performed a vanishing illusion instead. And the night before he died, Welles went on *The Merv Griffin Show* and did a card trick!

using big-stage illusions that required a lot of equipment. But other magicians took the road of Georges Méliès and worked on special effects for film illusions.[2] As special effects improved, the next century saw movies that ranged from exotic magical adventure (the 1940 *The Thief of Baghdad*) to science fiction (*Star Wars*, anyone?) to successful adaptations of fantasy books full of magic (*Harry Potter* and *The Lord of the Rings* movies ranked first and second at the box office in 2001). There have also been occasional movies about stage magicians, and of these, the best might be the 2006 film *The Prestige*.

Directed by Christopher Nolan (he also did *The Dark Knight* and *Batman Begins*), *The Prestige* reveals what a magic performance was like in the Victorian age. It also shows the professional and personal

---

2  *Despite his pioneering work, as an old man Méliès ended up selling newspapers in a train station. Brian Selznick's terrific book* The Invention of Hugo Cabret *is about this very subject.*

jealousies that magicians have always had with each other. These performers live in a world of magic espionage, with each conjuror anxious to keep his secrets secret while using spies and deception to learn the tricks of his rivals.

Among the illusions *The Prestige* explains is one called the Transported Man, in which a magician gets into a cabinet on one side of the stage and immediately gets out of another cabinet on the other side. How can it be done? I won't explain the movie's plot (which has three different solutions), but Houdini did a trick like this with his brother Hardeen. Houdini would go into one cabinet, and his look-alike brother would get out of the other. Harry Blackstone sometimes did the same thing with his brother, with the "real" Blackstone appearing at the back of the theater.

## Criss Angel

*RÉSUMÉ:* Goth-rock magician Criss Angel is best known as the star of the TV series *Mindfreak*. Born in 1967 as Christopher Sarantakos, he first got interested in magic when he was seven and his aunt showed him a magic trick. He was *Mindfreaked!* Or maybe just impressed.

Either way, when Angel was sixteen, he set the living room carpet on fire practicing with pyrotechnics, and not long afterward, he began performing at children's parties in New Jersey. Skill, ambition, and the fact that his mother mortgaged the family home to pay for it led him to star in a successful off Broadway stage show called *Mindfreak* in 2001, which led to his TV show. On the TV show, Angel was once run over by a Hummer while lying on a bed of nails. (I think it would have been more impressive if he'd been driving the Hummer when he did it.)

**TRADEMARK ILLUSIONS:** Angel seems equally interested in doing close-up magic, big illusions, and escape artistry. His close-up magic might be the best of these; he has diabolical skills.

**INSPIRATIONS:** Angel has a thing about Houdini. (Don't all magicians?) This inspired him to submerge himself in a water tank (while chained!) for twenty-four hours. He also has a thing about David Blaine—a bad thing. "I put the challenge out there, any day, anytime, anyplace, any challenge that [David Blaine] can dream up; let's do it side by side and let the people judge who is the true provocateur of the century."

**FUN FACT:** Angel's fans are called "The Loyal." (This is an improvement on my fan club: The Disappointed.)

*QUOTABLE:* "I wanted to prove to myself that first place isn't enough." Angel was referring to having four big fish-hooks stuck into his back so that a helicopter could lift him and fly around. (Not only does he take first place in that event, he also gets second, third, and fourth.)

*THE SHOW MIGHT GO ON:* In late 2008, Angel started a Las Vegas stage show with Cirque de Soleil called *Believe.* It was an uneasy mixture; a fan of both Angel and Cirque described it as having "Billy Idol sing the theme to NPR's *All Things Considered.*" Hopefully the show will improve; the contract is for Angel to perform the show 4,600 times! (And since he's "co-writer, illusions creator and designer, original concept creator and star," I don't think they can do it without him.)

# Merlin

## AND OTHER MAGIC MAKERS

*"WATCH WITH GLITTERING EYES THE WHOLE WORLD AROUND YOU BECAUSE THE GREATEST SECRETS ARE ALWAYS HIDDEN IN THE MOST UNLIKELY PLACES. THOSE WHO DO NOT BELIEVE IN MAGIC WILL NEVER FIND IT."* —Roald Dahl

Of all the legendary wizards of lore, there's one big-daddy mage holding his staff far above all others. **Merlin**! He was a kingmaker, a master of illusion, and a guy who really needed to shave. Merlin was the role model for the hordes of wise, all-seeing wizards who followed him. As the original Wise Old Man, he even set magical fashion for centuries, with his pointed cap, long beard, flowing robe, and staff. (Dude, Gandalf is a total poser!)

But whence came this most auspicious conjuror?

There apparently really was a Welsh poet in the 500s named Myrddin. He was an eccentric character who moved to the wilds of Scotland and made prophecies. A writer named Geoffrey of Monmouth dusted off Myrddin in 1135 and renamed him "Merlin" for his book *History of the Kings of Britain*. In Geoffrey's version, Merlin possessed such incredible skills, he'd transplanted Stonehenge from Ireland (where it was known as "Giant's Dance") to its current location on Salisbury Plain in England. (For the record, historians agree that Stonehenge was in its current location more than 2,500 years before the real Myrddin was born.)

## Light Saber = Magic Staff

He had a beard, wore a hooded robe, possessed mysterious powers, and taught a punk kid how to handle magic. I don't want to Force the comparison, but Obi-wan "Ben" Kenobi is a sci-fi Merlin!

Merlin's legend only grew over the years. An epic poem from the 1400s gave Merlin an enchantress for a mother and a demon for a father. (Just like me!) Merlin was then taught by a mage named Blaise to use his powers for good (yawn) instead of evil. As the wizard's skills developed, he was able to do impressive tricks like turning night into day, creating armies of phantoms, and correctly identifying the Knights of the Round Table in full armor.

Most importantly, Merlin had powers of prophecy, which allowed him to arrange the birth of Arthur. Following that success,

Merlin educated him and finally served as King Arthur's wizard-in-residence.

## Getting to the Point

Why do witches, wizards, and other people with secret knowledge wear pointy hats? To explain this, a man named John Duns Scotus came up with a theory. (Keep in mind this was about eight hundred years ago.) John *Duns* Scotus thought that a pointy hat could make a person *smarter*. The idea was that the point on the cap would *focus* the person's thoughts.

People who agreed with Duns started wearing pointy hats and were called *Dunsmen*. However, since it seemed like a silly idea, the pointy "Duns" cap soon became a symbol of *stupidity*, not intelligence. Eventually, in early American schools, the tradition of keeping a "dunce" cap for the worst students lasted all the way into the 1950s. (Too bad the hat didn't actually help them focus their thoughts.)

This is an important part of Merlin's schtick: playing the Wise Old Man who serves as advisor to a young apprentice. (BTW, "wizard" is an old English word that comes from "wise.")

Skipping ahead to more recent times, the legend of Merlin was a huge influence on an Oxford professor named J. R. R. Tolkien. (The J. R. R. stands for John Ronald Reuel.) Tolkien created the character of Gandalf for a book he wrote in the early 1930s titled *The Hobbit*. But Merlin wasn't the *only* wizard Tolkien was inspired by. He knew that Scandinavian lore tells of an ancient, powerful character named Väinämöinen. Tolkien went to the trouble of learning Finnish just so that he could read the stories about Väinämöinen in their original form.

NBA star Tim Duncan has a giant tattoo of Merlin on his back.

## Merlin Would Be Proud

A 1997 BBC poll named *The Lord of the Rings* the greatest literary work of the twentieth century.

Now *there* was an author who was serious about his magic!

*The Hobbit* and the following *Lord of the Rings* trilogy were popular, but it wasn't until the books were published in the United States in the 1960s that they turned into huge hits. Even the lesser-known wizards from the stories, like Saruman and Little Timmy, became well known. Suddenly everyone was wearing a "Gandalf for President" button and the image of a long-bearded wizard showed up on everything from rock albums to breakfast cereals.

The next great twist in wizardly literature was in 1997, when Harry Potter

## Say It Ain't So, Jo!

J. K. Rowling started but didn't finish reading *The Lord of the Rings*. (And she hasn't read all of the Narnia books either!)

made his debut. It was easy to see how this series kept Merlin's memory alive. Albus Dumbledore himself is a member of the Order of Merlin, as anyone who has ever received correspondence from him knows. (Hey, it's on his official letterhead.) And, of course, Dumbledore served as a Wise Old Man for Harry. But I'm guessing you may already be familiar with Harry Potter, yes?

To get back to Merlin's own story, it came to an end when the wizard was seduced by an enchantress named Vivien. She learned Merlin's secrets and then imprisoned him, either in a cave or an oak tree. Either way, the mighty sorcerer was never to return. (Verily, that sucks![1]) As for King Arthur, he had his own bad experience with a sorceress. After all, his sister, Morgana (a.k.a. Morgan le Fay), was one! Some (but not all) legends show her as a wicked schemer. She steals Arthur's sword, Excalibur, tries to destroy his kingdom, and sticks chewed gum on the inside of his crown.

This image of magical and dangerous women was around long before Merlin's legend. For example, the ancient Greeks wrote of the beautiful and deadly Circe, a woman so powerful she could turn men into woodpeckers and persuade whole forests to relocate. Her niece was Medea, who was also pretty intimidating. When the hero Jason (of Argonauts fame) dumped Medea for Creusa, the daughter of the king of Corinth, Medea did what

1  If you're interested, T. H. White wrote an excellent series with Merlin that starts with The Sword in the Stone (1938). The 1963 Disney film of the same name features a Wizards' Duel that might be good to review before your Magicians' Face-Off (see page 200).

any self-respecting sorceress would do. She killed Creusa and the king, and then she left town.

With so many great role models, why are there so few female magicians? Well, maybe with all the legends of their witchcraft and treachery, women got sick of the whole business. (And people do buy more magic kits for boys than girls.) Even so, women will always be linked with magic because men will always think women possess powers beyond their understanding. ("Mom, what's intuition?")

While there are multitudes of other wizards in fiction and folktale, two of my favorites are Prospero, from Shakespeare's *The Tempest*, and Rincewind, one of the many wizards in Terry Pratchett's *Discworld* series. But let me end by mentioning Oz, from L. Frank Baum's book *The Wizard of Oz*. It was published in 1900, and many other books followed in the series.

The Wizard in Oz doesn't actually have a name in the first book, but he is later revealed to be Oscar Zoroaster Phadrig Issac Norman Henkle Emmanuel Ambroise Diggs. He was originally a magician from Nebraska who performed as Oz. The magician put his name on everything, including his hot-air balloon. This proved convenient when Oz was whisked to the land of...Oz. The people there thought he was destined to be their leader!

If you've read the book or seen the movie, you know that Oz is actually a *magician*, NOT a wizard, and therefore, he is a fraud twice over. However, later in the series, he works as an apprentice for Glinda (the Good Witch!) and Oz does learn some real magic. (But try as he might, Oz couldn't grow a beard as cool as Merlin's.)

As for L. Frank Baum, he had some magic going for him, too. *The Wizard of Oz* was a huge hit. In fact, it was SUCH a hit that Baum wrote thirteen more Oz books. Though none would do as well as the original, Baum had yet another success he could point to: The Oz books were the first American fairy tales, and the Wizard of Oz was *nothing* like Merlin, nor his British descendents, Gandalf and Dumbledore.

Score one for originality!

## *Enchanted Stick Profile Page*

*NAME:* Magic Wand

*RÉSUMÉ:* A magic wand (or for mature conjurors, the magic staff) has symbolized the channeling of magical forces since time immemorial. Why a wand? One theory is that early weapons like clubs and spears evolved into ceremonial forms. That's why a king had his scepter and a magician had his wand. (Me? I have a big toothbrush.)

*EARLY ADOPTERS:* While wands can be